13 REASONS
TO GIVE A DAMN
IN 2016

Brian Bosché

Published by BeReadyMEDIA, LLC.
Printed in the United States of America.

LISTEN FREE!

Listen to Brian Bosché read the Introduction...

"Ready to Rise? It's Time To Give A Damn."

AND... Chapter 1...

"Give A Damn... Because We're America The Broken"

Go to...

13ReasonsToGiveADamn.com

RIGHT NOW!

To my Creator...
For the blessings of life, grace, vision, and talent.

To my bride, Gabrielle Bosché...
For being a powerful source of inspiration and restoration.
For being my greatest helper.

To my parents, Neal & Kimberly Bosché...
For cultivating the pursuit of vision and excellence.
For pushing me beyond excuses.

To my sister, Lauren Rocco...
For faithful, unending spiritual support.
For the cover art of this book.

To my brother and right-hand man, Tyler Lucas...
For his commitment, intelligence, common sense, and excellence.
For the well-reviewed research in this book.

To my mentor, Tamara Lowe...
For demonstrating excellence in business and friendship.
For setting the very best example in mentorship.

To my grandmother, Katherine Walton...
For providing endless edits and insight.
For getting me addicted to coffee.

To my grandmother, Jean Bosché...
For inspiring a passion for politics.
For inspiring a love for talk radio.

Advanced Praise For
13 REASONS TO GIVE A DAMN IN 2016

"Brian embodies what today's America needs: A conservative opinion without the grey hair, but the intelligence and desire to see America become greater than ever before."

Tamara Holder, FOX News Channel Contributor

"Brian Bosché is an up-and-coming media powerhouse. New York Times Bestselling Author. A-List Speaker. Primetime Television Commentator. These are titles that will follow his name. Sometimes we get a glimpse into the future. We get to see who will fill the shoes of Limbaugh, Beck, and Hannity. Brian is the future."

Tamara Lowe, NYT Bestselling Author of "Get Motivated!"

"Brian Bosché has a vision that Americans from across the spectrum will appreciate. He's a patriot in the finest sense of the word and this book is exactly what this generation of patriots crave. It's common sense without the spin."

Brandon & Jared Vallorani, Liberty Alliance

TABLE OF REASONS TO GIVE A DAMN

Ready To Rise?
It's Time To Give A Damn.

Thankfully, my phone is lying next to my head. I am on the floor. My mind is spinning. The tears are unstoppable and oxygen evades me. I can feel the carpet on my cheek and the sweat on my skin. In an instant, I am on the floor destroyed. One phone call from my wife of one year took me from standing to nothing. It was unfair, but in mere minutes my marriage was over. There was no getting it back. The sound of my own crying shatters the peace of an empty home in the mountains of Roanoke, Virginia. It is the week of Independence Day 2013.

At the time, I was a national investigative reporter for Glenn Beck's television network, TheBlaze, but I was off that week. I had joined TheBlaze after graduating from law school. While a reporter, I covered stories on radical Islamic terrorism and government corruption. As for the week of Independence Day, my family was vacationing at the beach. I didn't go. Instead, I remained in Roanoke trying to save what was already dead. From the floor, I couldn't see much through the blur of tears. It had been a long day. I'd always thought emotions of this kind were fake, and the result of someone seeking attention. Yet here, I was overcome with these very emotions. Was help on the way?

My iPhone lit-up. It was a call from my sister, Lauren. She had no idea what she was about to hear. With a shaky hand, I answered and put it on speakerphone. Holding the phone was impossible. When I opened my mouth, there was no hello—just a cry for help. I'm not sure Lauren said anything, but the phone quickly changed hands. Mom was on the line. I couldn't comprehend what she was saying, just that she was trying to talk me down. Nothing worked. My only response was more tears. Five hours away, she was worried. She wanted the family to drive back to Roanoke. I finally spoke a word. "No!" I screamed back. Dad had another solution. Help was on the way...

I can't help but compare my brokenness to America's brokenness. She too has fallen to the floor—cracked from the inside out. Once again, her people stand divided along lines of race and class. Violent protests fill her streets. Her leaders were once visionaries. They were the keepers of our Republic. Now, out of self-interest, they feed on what's left of her. She lies economically destitute. Her marketplace stands on a crumbling foundation. Her creditors won't stop calling and she craves innovative minds to revive her. Her walls are no stronger than that of thatch and mud. Enemies stand ready to burn her down—from the outside and the inside. She has faith, but it wanes. Shining city on a hill? Hardly. Her preeminence in the next century is questionable. Is help on the way?

Help stepped into my Virginia home in the midst of a dark divorce; and with it, the beginning of personal restoration. A

2

trusted friend of the family found me on the floor that day. My muscles were so tight that I felt I needed to be pried open. It took some time for me to breathe normally again. That first full breath began a change in my view of brokenness. I had always believed our Creator endowed us with "certain unalienable rights." After all, that's what Thomas Jefferson told me.

I had also believed that our Creator crafted us with unique gifts and talents, but I had never recognized His refining power through adversity. In February of 2014—seven months after being helped up off the floor—I took a step of faith and left TheBlaze to aggressively build a supersized new brand of political commentary.

Personal brokenness prepared me for a radical season of growth that led to these very pages. These pages are meant to equip you. Each chapter will arm you with the knowledge, wisdom, and reasons to give a damn in 2016. You'll be able to navigate the political headlines as the presidential election season heats up. You'll see past the superficial and look for principles. More importantly, you'll be able band together with your fellow Americans to channel our country's brokenness towards her restoration.

Truthfully, we all harbor some kind of brokenness. It may be a dark past, deep depression, loss, or addiction. Perhaps you've experienced a divorce, a failure in business, or a betrayal that cut to the core. Brokenness is our greatest strength and the source of trial-tested wisdom. Like each of us individually, America is broken, but not irreparably. Brokenness has readied our nation to step out of the ashes. I believe our greatest days could be ahead, but that's up to us. We are the phone next to America's head. We are her friend at the door. Ready to help America? It's time to give a damn.

- 1 -

Give A Damn...
Because We're America The Broken

The projected outcome was dismal. One decision in New Hampshire would place the very existence of the United States in question. As President of the New England state, John Langdon had seen the numbers: 30 to 77. It wasn't going to pass. America's Constitution was facing its first defeat—one that could bring further setbacks. Eight of the 13 states had already accepted and ratified it. Nine states were required to make the Constitution effective for the entire nation.[1]

But the dismal prediction in New Hampshire was the result of division over the draft. The vulnerable Constitution was meant to provide America with a centralized government and a strong, national defense. That it did. But the folks in New Hampshire were concerned. For them, the document didn't adequately protect their individual freedoms. Their concern was valid, but the key question was whether that could be solved later. After all, the Constitution allowed for changes by amendment.[2]

Langdon was frustrated. Would his state risk America's future? Would New Hampshire reject a document that provided a solution for its concerns? They had sacrificed so much.

Langdon himself was all in from the beginning. He was a patriot.

Two years before the Declaration of Independence, he declared himself a traitor to Britain when he helped seize British military supplies from a base in Portsmouth. Langdon failed to sign the Declaration because he was fighting alongside militiamen. And when New Hampshire was unwilling to send delegates to the Constitutional Convention, Langdon paid not just for himself, but also for his colleague Nicholas Gilman.[3]

If anyone remembered the cry for independence, the bloodshed, the debt, and the sacrifice to achieve victory, it was Langdon. This was bigger than any one state. The war was over. America had won united, but she stood broken on the ledge of history. Disagreements over the Constitution's text were understandable, but perhaps Langdon knew that coming together was more important. New Hampshire could have left America as a fractured nation, but divisions were set aside. Back then, the things that mattered prevailed. Vision prevailed. America found strength through her brokenness. The vote was 57 to 47! It passed.[4]

On the eve of the 2016 Presidential Election, this is true: The things that unite America have not prevailed. Langdon would certainly be disappointed. Look at what we've done. We've created an overly sensitive environment of political correctness and complacent brokenness. In fact, we're so sensitive and politically correct that our national conversation has become shallow and superficial.

For example, I'm a Christian—albeit a largely imperfect one. I guarantee the mere mention of my faith might have made some readers uncomfortable. In fact, some reading this are already irritated that I had the audacity to even mention my faith. After all, I did use the word "damn" in the title of this book.

At what point did we, as a society, become so sensitive? When did America become the political equivalent of a church mouse? Why can't we be comfortable with disagreement and robust debate—and still leave the table as friends? After all, we cherish the First Amendment, right?

Essentially, I'm saying that America as a whole, and we as individuals, lack the strength, depth, and authenticity that we certainly possess at our core. We watch television and browse the web to gas-up on plug-n-play arguments that I'm not even sure we believe. Or, we watch and browse to escape. Forget politics.

The bottom line is that we are afraid to show our true selves. We're afraid to be honest; and we run from debate and the battle of ideas. Our political pundits scream from the sidelines hoping to viscerally tear each other apart over the smallest of non-issues. That's brokenness. We're better than that.

Now most of this has been the result of irresponsible leadership and irrational rhetoric. Our sense of respect, civility, and love for one another is virtually gone. Common resolve towards the big picture—like in Langdon's time—doesn't exist. More than anything, our "leaders" in Washington lack entirely in vision. They're nothing more than power brokers pursuing shortsighted victories—victories that achieve little to preserve our nation's future.

In 2014, Republicans took the Senate from Democrats, who had been in control since 2007.[5] For the first time since President Obama took office, Republicans controlled both the House and the Senate. After the victory, the new Senate majority leader, Mitch McConnell (R-KY), told Fox News' Megyn Kelly that "not mess[ing] up the playing field" for the 2016 Republican nominee for president was "probably the best we can hope for."[6] Wow, Mitch. That's it? Hope?

> **"Our political pundits scream from the sidelines hoping to viscerally tear each other apart over the smallest of non-issues. That's brokenness. We're better than that."**

I remember watching that segment on a treadmill in my hometown gym. I nearly fell off the treadmill. And if John Langdon had been running beside me, he might have felt the same. I remember thinking, "That's the best we've got—the best we can 'hope' for?"

I couldn't believe it. Between Leader McConnell and House Speaker, John Boehner (R-OH), Republicans had taken control of one-third of the United States government. This was their moment. This was their chance to boldly present their case to the American people—the opportunity to cast vision and cast it big. If it were a court of law, this was their opening statements—their time to make a splash. They flopped and floundered, like a dying fish on a blistering hot dock "hoping" to land back in the water. They had achieved "victory" and didn't know what to do with it. That's brokenness. That's "politics as usual."

2016 doesn't have to be that way. Politics as usual has disheartened we the American voters. Why should we care? There's nothing inspiring coming from the top. The "leadership" is lackluster. There is no inspiring message. There is no uniting vision and lack of vision is precisely the problem.

In 2008, then-Senator Obama's message of "hope" and "change" was empty—shallow at best. In reality, it was subpar. His message was a glittering generality that meant absolutely nothing. That's not vision. Vision paints the picture of an inspiring outcome; and the message of that vision charts the path to achieve the outcome. The message is overwhelming, powerful, and ultimately achieves victory in the battle of ideas. In lest you think I am harping on liberals or "Obama-bashing," I say unabashedly that conservatives have failed to provide inspiring leadership as well. Now this book is not about President Obama or any 2016 candidate. In fact, I've done my best to rid the mention of any candidate from these pages. This isn't about the horse race or who's going to win. This is about moving from brokenness to restoration, from divided to united, and from hope to vision.

> **"This isn't about the horse race or who's going to win. This is about moving from brokenness to restoration, from divided to united, and from hope to vision."**

America was birthed by visionaries. Vision is in our DNA. Those in Washington, D.C.—whether purposely or not—have worked to undermine it, but vision is not foreign to us. Let us take it for a spin. During his fourth presidential debate against then-Vice President, Richard Nixon, John F. Kennedy said this:

> *"I think we have to demonstrate to the people of the world that we're determined in this free country of ours to be first – not first if – not first but – not first when – but first. And when we are strong and when we are first, then freedom gains; then the prospects for peace increases; then the prospects for our society gain."*[7]

Kennedy's vision was simple—that America should be strong and first among all nations. It was declarative and unbending. Through powerful communication, Kennedy also laid the path to victory. America would not make excuses. There would be no ifs, ands, or buts about it. His message had cadence and momentum. It was overwhelming, powerful, and ultimately achieved victory over Vice President Nixon in the battle of ideas.

As America's Civil War was coming to a close, President Abraham Lincoln said this in his second inaugural address:

"… [L]et us strive on to finish the work we are in, to bind up the nation's wounds … to do all which may achieve and cherish a just and lasting peace among ourselves and with all nations."[8]

Lincoln captured the moment. America had suffered great loss. Battlefields were drenched with the crimson blood of young men. Lincoln's desired outcome was not merely to bring the war to a close. His words forged the vision for lasting peace. Like Kennedy, he laid the path. Finish the job, come together, and bind-up the nation's wounds. John Langdon would have been proud. That is what vision looks like. Yet in today's context, it feels uncomfortable, weird, and… well… oddly refreshing.

The question now becomes how to do it again and how to do it markedly better. Quoting past visionaries doesn't make us visionaries—neither does quoting history. Those who don't know history are doomed to repeat it, but those who live in the past are doomed to sit back and fail to define the future.

We don't need another Lincoln, Kennedy, or even another Reagan. I'm sorry, but they're dead and quoting them unfortunately won't bring them back. Their principles were powerful and should not be forgotten, but unless we take what they said, make it our own, and apply it today, we're nothing more than walking quote banks—fashioned in the form of old, dusty libraries. We're no different than the guy who quotes TED Talks, but fails to execute change in his own life.

We need vision and leadership like we've never had before. We need a president who eclipses the capabilities of those who've come before—including George Washington. We expect the best from of our leaders and ourselves. How is this going to happen? How are we going to mark a change on Washington and our country in 2016? Very simply. As individuals, we must change first. The shift will not come from the top. Seriously. It won't.

> **"Quoting past visionaries doesn't make us visionaries—neither does quoting history. Those who don't know history are doomed to repeat it, but those who live in the past are doomed to sit back and fail to define the future."**

Government doesn't make itself smaller and politicians don't voluntarily move to places of discomfort. The shift I speak of must be enacted by we the American voters. We've all heard the phrase "sunlight is the best disinfectant." That's a lie. Many things occur in broad daylight and go unaddressed. The issue— whether in darkness or light—is who's watching? Who's armed with the best knowledge? Who possesses the greater vision? Sunlight is not the best disinfectant. Knowledge and a renewed vision within the American voter is.

It's easy to blame the politicians. "The System" is our go-to villain of choice. But truthfully, we are somewhat to blame. We allowed this atmosphere of political brokenness to percolate. We haven't armed ourselves with the knowledge and individual vision to be the shift, but we can! It's time for a heart change. Our choice to do so will set the example and start the necessary shift—a grassroots transformation from a generation of Americans willing to give a damn!

What looms ahead is a long, rough path. That's not fear mongering or exaggeration. That's honesty. But know this: a heart change on the part of every American will shorten our path to restoration and begin a catalytic change across the America political landscape. Bring your vision to the battlefield of ideas. Change starts with you.

Give A Damn... Because We're America The Broken

- 2 -

Give A Damn...
Because The Ruling Class Is Classless

She had expected a normal trip to the mailbox. It was the last week in June of 2014 on a warm summer day. There couldn't have been much more than bills and coupons for the next trip to the store. Just like the walk you and I take to check the mail, hers wasn't much different. She noticed the same old cracks in the driveway and whether the grass needed a trim. Like always, the neighbors had parked their cars just the same. It was another day in the neighborhood and another day since her husband, Doug Chase, had been gone. Suzanne Chase reached the mailbox. She had no idea that opening it would turn a simple walk into a shattered, angry heart. Among the bills and coupons, there was a letter from the Bedford, Massachusetts Veterans Affairs (VA) Hospital. For what? Why? What could it possibly be about?

Doug had fought in Vietnam. Deaf in one ear, calling him up for service should have been illegal, but Vermont was behind on their draft numbers. So he was called-up anyway, pulling him away from a promising career. Doug experienced much of what the Vietnam War had to offer. He was exposed to "Agent Orange"—a toxic herbicide that the U.S. had used to kill vegetation that provided cover to the enemy. Agent Orange has since been linked to numerous cancers. His time in Vietnam also left him with lifelong, post-traumatic stress disorder (PTSD).

Fast forward to 2011. Doug was experiencing pounding headaches and struggled to walk. In June of the same year, a trip to the doctor confirmed that he had stage four cancer and two brain tumors the size of a plum. His disease was aggressive.

By April of 2012, he was a paraplegic. It had spread to his lungs, bladder, and skin. Worse, the cancer was eating away at his spine. Now the hospital where Doug received treatments was an hour away in Boston. The trip required a special ambulance and back brace to reduce the pain of bumps in the road. Eventually, the ride became unbearable. Doug needed a hospital that was closer to home. The only choice was the nearby VA Hospital in Bedford, Massachusetts.

> **"By April of 2012, he was a paraplegic. It had spread to his lungs, bladder, and skin. Worse, the cancer was eating away at his spine."**

In my conversation with Suzanne, she said that when Doug left the Army, he wanted nothing to do with the VA. He felt that "nothing good came out of the VA." His actions backed-up the feeling. For his entire post-Vietnam life and before his cancer diagnosis, Doug had never applied for VA benefits. But when the long ambulance ride became too uncomfortable, Suzanne helped him apply for care at the Bedford VA. It was the last resort, but necessary. He was in too much pain. However, Doug never got an appointment. He and Suzanne had no idea that they were victims of bureaucratic corruption—a scheduling and bonus scandal that was ripping through the entire VA System. That was in February of 2012.

By August, cancer was ready to take him. According to Suzanne, the last few weeks were wretched. His brain had deteriorated so much that he had forgotten the faces of friends and family, and the 40 years that he had lived in Massachusetts. He died August 20, 2012. Doug never received a single treatment from the Bedford VA hospital. Given Doug's veteran status, Suzanne called on the VA once again. This time, it was for funeral benefits. She was denied. The basis? The VA said that Doug had never received treatments from the system. How ironic.

Now, two years later on a warm summer day, she was opening a letter from the Bedford VA. Good news. They wanted Doug to schedule an appointment "promptly." I guess they were a little late. The spoils of corruption come at a price. Sometimes, the price is death.

Corruption is the sludge that halts America's pursuit of excellence; so is incompetence. Laughably, the result of corruption and incompetence isn't much different. Each creates setbacks, failures, and threats to our security. Each put the we the American voter in harm's way. But there is a key difference between the two.

By definition, incompetence is "the inability to do something successfully."[1] As for me, incompetence is the willful ignorance of true excellence and what achieving it requires. By definition, corruption is "dishonest or fraudulent conduct by those in power."[2] As for me, corruption is the willful betrayal of the American people. No matter the definition, both corruption and incompetence are unacceptable. There is no place in our society for such foolishness. But at the VA, such foolishness ran wild — resulting in the dastardly breach of our trust and likely the premature death of Doug Chase and many others.

> **"The spoils of corruption come at a price.**
> **Sometimes, the price is death."**

The VA hospital system exists to care for our nation's veterans. As with most government-run agencies, the system is full of red tape. To incentivize efficiency, patient wait times were once tied to VA employees' bonuses and pay raises.[3] The idea was to offer an incentive to provide prompt medical care. However, the bonuses incentivized lying and resulted in death.

In Phoenix, Arizona alone, CNN reported that "at least 40 veterans died while waiting for appointments." Also according to the report, the patients were on a secret list designed to hide the delays.[4] Since the severe delays were hidden from official reports, overall wait times looked fine and VA officials got paid. The Phoenix VA director, Sharon Helman, received an $8,495 bonus. After an investigation, the bonus was taken back.[5] The VA Scandal serves as an example of bureaucratic corruption—the willful betrayal of the American people by *unelected*, unaccountable officials. Let me reiterate, the scandal killed people. That was the price. Suzanne Chase knew the price, saw the price, and ultimately felt the price. To her, it was more than a bonus. It was real.

There is another kind of corruption—the kind where *elected* officials betray the American people. Political corruption. It's the kind of betrayal that slaps every American voter in the face and says, "I'm above the law." There is one problem with that. In our system of government, no one—not even the President of the United States—is above the law. Period. Every single person is to play by the same rules. The best example is a simple one, but let me first reiterate: this book is not about any 2016 candidate. I don't seek to endorse or analyze any candidate's chance of winning. Today, our country is too focused on parties, candidates, and labels—when the focus should be on principles.

The most recent example of political corruption is the Hillary Clinton email scandal. During her entire time as Secretary of State, Clinton used personal email addresses—mixing personal and government business. She said the choice was made out of "convenience"—claiming that she didn't want to carry two phones.[6] Do not forget that this was someone who dealt with top secret information. Also remember that federal law requires all government emails to be kept and recorded. More than that, know that Clinton and her personal staff had sole control over the server where the email was hosted.[7]

After Clinton's use of personal email addresses for government business came to light, who determined what was government business? Congress? Nope. The State Department? Wrong again. Ladies and gentlemen, Hillary Clinton. Yes. She decided. Her staff decided. And when the review was done, the server was wiped clean.[8] Gone. It was the willful betrayal of the American People. Cover-up or not, we'll never know what was really on the server.

Why was it done that way? According to one of her aids, anything that "pertained" to Clinton's work was turned over to the State Department. However, "If she emailed with her daughter about flower arrangements for her wedding, that didn't go in."[9] After all, that's private. At first, you might agree with that logic. Why should she have to turn over her private emails? Here's why: Clinton's actions demonstrate that same "above the law" mentality.

> **"Much like cancer had eaten away at the spine of Doug Chase, the cancer of corruption has eaten away at the spine of vision and virtue in American leadership."**

She would say that the personal email addresses were hers. Therefore, it was okay for her to choose what to release. She is dead wrong and potentially broke federal law. Remember, who made the choice? She did. She chose to use personal email. She chose to mix personal with sensitive, government business. Therefore, she had no right to oversee the release of the emails. Clinton made her daughter's wedding government business— not the other way around. It is Congress and the State Department that should have conducted the review.

Bureaucratic and political corruption hasn't only gummed-up our government. Each is an active threat to our freedom and security—and sometimes our lives. Much like cancer had eaten away at the spine of Doug Chase, the cancer of corruption has eaten away at the spine of vision and virtue in American leadership. America once served as the greatest example of republican democracy in all of human history. Now, we're failing miserably. Our country's leaders are backsliding and ruining the very example we so powerfully set. Suzanne Chase thinks our nation's culture of corruption is sickening.

"I don't think anybody knows what the hell they're doing. The news used to be depressing, now it's just frightening. I think I would like to leave this earth feeling that there were good, intelligent people running this country. It doesn't feel like we've learned from the past. It feels like we've turned a blind eye to corruption in Washington," she said.

The question becomes, how do we stop the backsliding? How do we set a new example? We don't have to bear the cost of our leaders' corrupt actions. America needs a return to vision and virtue. Perhaps Suzanne knows what that looks like. When I asked her if she received any compensation from the VA for her and her husband's pain, she said:

> *"No, but I'd rather any money they would give me go to a widowed young mother of our nation's veterans. It worries me that they're not getting cared for."*

As individuals, that's the kind of heart we must have to clean up the cancer of corruption in America.

- 3 -

Give A Damn...
Because The Power Of Wisdom Lay Forgotten

*NPR: "Spending Bill Passes,
Just Hours Before Deadline."*

If Congress were a student, it would be the student who busts through a professor's door two minutes before the deadline on a big assignment. We all knew the person who pulled an all-nighter on a 20-page paper. They hadn't slept and kept themselves going with espresso and Red Bull. Shower? Please. There's no time. Twenty pages? Does 19.5 count? Is it possible to increase the font size or widen the margins without the professor noticing? Do you have printer? USB stick? Folder? Remember this panicked moment? "I LITERALLY have like 20 minutes to turn this thing in and it's going to take ten minutes to walk there! Really! Does your printer work?!

Sound familiar? What's funny is that we all know the Congress that has pulled all-nighters on bills to keep our government "funded." They slept all snuggly while their staffers ran on espresso and Red Bull. Twenty pages? How about 1,600? Read *War and Peace* for inspiration. Is it possible to add more spending? More projects? More salaries? More benefits?

More endangered species? Absolutely. Does the printer have ink? Will it fit on a USB stick? How about this panicked moment? "We LITERALLY have only a couple of hours to vote on this thing!"

Back in December of 2014, that is essentially what happened. By midnight on December 11, Congress needed to pass a spending bill to keep the federal government working and funded through September 2015.[1] I guess you could say December 11 was the bill's "due date." Were they proactive? No. Did they start the process early? No. Did they look to shrink our national debt ($18.1 trillion at the time of this writing[2])? No. Did they avoid wasteful spending? No. Did they wait till the last minute because of sharp political divisions? Yes. Did they approach the bill and America's future with wisdom? No and that was the problem.

Wisdom would have been proactive. Wisdom would have sought ways to reduce the nation's debt. Wisdom would have laid aside short-sighted political divisions. Wisdom would have passed the bill well before the deadline. But wisdom did not prevail. Idiocy prevailed on both sides. Neither side won and America lost big. The bill passed with less than three hours to go before the deadline.

It promised over $1 trillion in new spending and contained hundreds of millions of dollars in wasteful spending.[3] It also included funding for a group called ACORN—which closed its doors in 2010 amid scandal.[4] Finally, no one read the bill and worse, not a single page of the legislation addressed America's dismal financial future. At the current pace, America's national debt could exceed $33 trillion in less than 10 years.[5]

Speaker of the House, John Boehner (R-OH), said, "We've done this in a bipartisan fashion, and frankly it's a good bill."[6] Speaker Boehner must have left his brain back in his office. His "final paper" was a last minute, unread, bipartisan betrayal of we the American voter and our future. Both Boehner and the rest of Congress lacked a key requirement of leadership. Wisdom.

In America, we celebrate the First Amendment. It secures our God-given right to freely express ourselves without the threat of government punishment.[7] For those who want it, knowledge and wisdom is freely available. Here the battlefield of ideas can thrive in our robust representative republic. This environment allows for a steady flow of information. Technology has only increased the flow to that of fire hose. Given the 24-hour news cycle, YouTube, countless information sites, and social media, lack of information is not our country's problem. As a nation, we're lacking wisdom, but we can change that.

What is wisdom and why is it important? Wisdom is the combination of knowledge, life experience, and good judgment.[8] At its core, wisdom finds its foundation in principle—not book smarts or even common sense. Intellect and common sense are important, but wisdom is powerful because wisdom is tested by experience. No leader or individual can expect to cast the right vision or make good decisions without wisdom.

Our leaders in Washington take an oath to preserve, protect, and defend the Constitution. Carrying out that duty requires wisdom. As voters, we don't swear an oath, but to protect our nation, we must bear the same responsibility.

Because what happens when the folks we elected have gone astray—like they have today? What happens when they fail—like they did with the spending bill? Who is supposed to be the backstop? Who is the last line of defense? We are. Thomas Jefferson said

"[W]henever things get so far wrong as to attract [the people's attention], [the people] may be relied on to set [things right]."[9]

Ask yourself this: Have things gone so far wrong as to attract your attention? Is $18.1 trillion dollars in debt enough? Is hundreds of millions of dollars in wasteful spending of your hard earned money enough? Is a mediocre, last minute Congress enough?

If it is enough, can you be relied on to "set things right?" Are you willing to arm yourself with the necessary wisdom? If you aren't sure, will you at least join hands with others and be a force of wisdom—a force of restoration. Will you help set the example for leaders who have gone astray? Being responsible for setting your country in the right direction may be intimidating. Perhaps you feel that you don't have the wisdom to be "relied on" or maybe you feel that America is too far-gone. I wouldn't blame you, but it doesn't have to be that way.

I want to encourage you and make this simple. The problem is not America's large debt or who is in charge. Forget the numbers and the ineffective leadership. Don't let them intimidate you. The real problem is a lack of wisdom. The problem is what happens before the result, before the debt, and before the vote.

> **"The real problem is a lack of wisdom. The problem is what happens before the result, before the debt, and before the vote."**

America lacks knowledge paired with life experience and good judgment. That bears repeating. America lacks knowledge paired with life experience and good judgment. It is truly that simple; and the solution is a simple choice. Choose wisdom. Arm yourself. Set the example for those in Washington. Let me show you how. Today, nearly every American has some sort of internet access. For all practical purposes, the internet connects you to everything you could ever need to know. For most, access is not the issue. The issue is what information you choose to read and who it comes from. Notice that it is "who" the information comes and not "where."

People distribute information based upon their knowledge and experience. Knowledge and experience impacts if, when, why, and how people distribute information. Don't believe me? Think about the last time you made a big announcement on social media. Remember when you went from "single" to "in a relationship"? What about the other way around? Think about how you announced your last promotion. You first considered "if" you would tell anyone. Then you thought about "when" and "why" you would tell them. Most certainly, you thought about "how" you would do it. The same is true for those who run news and information websites—and for those who write books.

The second issue is about what information you choose to read and retain. Why? Because information only becomes knowledge when you read it, understand its relevancy, and decide it is worth retaining. So make your choice wisely. Remember: knowledge is not a gift. You can acquire it, but it takes action. When you acquire it, combine it with your life experience and good judgment. You'll be a big step ahead of most in Washington.

There is one more thing to understand when choosing to arm yourself with wisdom. Social media and the internet provide immense access to information, but is often lacking context. In most cases, it is impossible to understand the depth or context of a headline posted on Twitter. One hundred forty characters are barely enough to post the headline itself. Like choosing wisdom, we must choose depth. We must choose to understand the context of the information we read. Sometimes that means digging deeper and comparing stories to other stories. Perhaps it means asking more questions.

If you leave with one thing, choose to arm yourself with wisdom. Combine the knowledge you acquire with your life experience and good judgment. Seek depth and context. Look past the 140-character tweets and 30-second sound bites. And if it helps, know that choosing wisdom will take you closer to understanding the truth. When wisdom becomes a way of life for you and me, we can be "relied on to set things right." Setting the example and setting things right starts within in your heart. You have to care. You have to give a damn.

Give A Damn... Because The Power Of Wisdom Lay Forgotten

- 4 -

Give A Damn...
Because Our Economy Craves Innovative Minds

She came into the world at age three. She had goals and dreams in her heart, but there was a system in place. Growing up as a child and later as a woman, she could have found love and encouragement in her parents. But wait, there was a system in place. Her dreams could have taken her to the top of medicine, business, law, education, government, or the arts. But there was a system in place. When it came time for college, she could have decided how to invest in her future. But there was a system in place. She could have shopped around for the best rate on student loans, but there was a system in place.

She could have tested her skills and talents in an economy where she was free to fail and succeed. But there was a system in place. After finding her way towards building a successful life, she could have invested freely to prepare for the future. But there was a system in place. And after all she had worked for— after all she had achieved—she could have left the fruits of her labor to her family. But there was a system in place. She was put into the ground at age 67. In her economy, there was a system in place from cradle to grave.

Her name was Julia. She was "born" in May of 2012 at the age of three. Her parents were the reelection staff for President Obama's second term campaign.[1] She had no face, no parents, and from age three to 67, everything that she needed to live was provided for. At age three, there was a free Head Start program. In her 20s, there were government-subsidized, low-interest loans to pay for expensive college tuition. Later, there was a government-backed, Small Business Administration loan to start her business. There was a lot of free stuff, but no indication as to how it was paid for. Julia's life was played-out in a pastel, two-dimensional computer environment. Her feet never moved. She was helpless and always looking to her left—in the direction of all that she had been given.

Julia was the Obama campaign's example of how big government "solutions" could make for a better life; and give a "better shot" towards being successful in an "unfair" economy. But the focus of the entire example was all about the *system* and nothing about the *individual*. It was about what the system could do and not what Julia could do with her talents and dreams. It disparaged capitalism and the individual freedom to take risks and succeed. Julia lived her life in an economy built on big government. In her world, neither the economy or the system cared about innovations that existed in her mind— innovations that could have been used to drive America forward. She didn't have parents because the government was there. She lived the motionless and expressionless life of a pawn ushered through a process.

According to the Obama campaign, Julia's life was amazing. Now Julia wasn't real, but the system was and it's alive and well today. Of greatest concern, the system has caused our government to spend trillions more than it takes in; and has pumped trillions into a stock market that is nothing short of artificial. It has brought about large expansions in the size of our government. A massive increase in regulations has stifled our job market and made it near impossible to start a business. Ultimately, the system has hindered our ability to improve our economic status and destroyed America's economic prowess on the world stage.

Our economy is in a hole. For well over a decade, the United States government has consistently spent more than it takes in. That's called deficit spending. Because of that, we've seen our national debt climb to more than $18 trillion. More than likely, it will rise above $20 trillion by the time President Obama leaves office and over $30 trillion within the next decade.[2] Now the President can claim that deficit spending went down under his watch. According to The Heritage Foundation however, if he and Congress continue to sit back, America will return to spending $1 trillion more than it takes in every single year.[3] Does that make you give a damn?

Maybe you watch the news everyday. Perhaps you pick up a newspaper at the local coffee shop every now and then. If that's how you keep track of the daily headlines, you may know that America's unemployment rate is 5.5% (at the time of this writing).[4] In his 2015 State of the Union Address, President

Obama said, "Our unemployment rate is now lower than it was before the [2008] financial crisis."[5] The President loves that percentage. So does the news media. When the updated percentage is released each month, it often makes the headlines. But the unemployment rate doesn't paint the whole picture. The full picture is one that President Obama and others never talk about.

Let's talk about a very simplified version of how the President's favorite percentage is calculated. First, imagine a pool of individuals who are actively participating in the job market. These folks are currently employed or unemployed, but are actively seeking jobs. Basically, that is the pool from which rate is determined. Simply divide the number of unemployed, active job seekers by the total number of active participants and multiply the result by 100. For example, let's say 1,000,000 people are actively participating in the job market. They are either employed or unemployed, active job seekers. Now, let's say 55,000 fall into the unemployed, active job seeker category. Divide 55,000 by 1,000,000 and you get 0.055. Multiply that by 100 and you get 5.5%—the President's favorite number.

Notice something? That calculation doesn't account for individuals who want a job, but have *given up* on their search. Those individuals are no longer "participating" in the job market—so they're not counted. But when you factor in those who have *given up*, the President's favorite number is less appealing at 10.9% (at the time of this writing).[6] Essentially, that means 1 out of 10 Americans who want a job can't find one. That result is the product of burdensome, big government systems and regulations. Does that make you give a damn?

Let's take a broader look. Unless you watch Fox Business Channel or CNBC, you may have never heard of "Quantitative Easing" or "QE." Though it may sound like Quantum Physics, it's not. Put simply, it is a monetary policy by which the United States Federal Reserve Bank floods financial institutions with money to increase lending and liquidity.[7] It does so by creating electronic money, which has a side effect of devaluing the U.S. dollar.[8] The simple definition of liquidity is the ability to convert an asset to cash quickly. In stock terms, it is the ability to quickly sell a stock for cash. A high level of stock trading activity would characterize a period of *increased* liquidity.[9]

When the future of our economy is uncertain, lending and liquidity generally goes down. As a result, our stock market often slows, home buying decreases, and our consumer spending subsides. The unemployment rate usually goes up.[10] After the 2008 financial crash, the Federal Reserve tried Quantitative Easing to speed up America's recovery.[11] By October 2014 when the program was stopped, the Federal Reserve "printed" nearly $4.5 trillion.[12] Some said it was a band aid that put off another crash—one that may have been necessary to reset our economy back to its true value. That's because flooding financial institutions with capital can encourage irresponsible lending.[13] In part, irresponsible lending led to the 2008 crash. Despite trying to speed-up America's recovery and prevent another crash, the Federal Reserve may have put off the inevitable and, in the process, given you less bang for your buck. Does that make you give a damn?

Now pair less bang for your buck with less opportunity to get ahead—to go farther than your parents did. The President and Democratic leaders on Capitol Hill like minority leader, Nancy Pelosi (D-CA), continue to talk about income inequality and growing the middle class.[14] In fact, the majority of President Obama's 2015 State of the Union address focused on those two issues. There were also more than a few mentions about an artificial increase in the minimum wage. Each of those suggestions is the wrong focus and short-sighted. Why grow just one class? And why stop at the middle class? Forget about "classes." Why not focus on Americans' ability to improve their economic status beyond that of the previous generation—to increase their "economic mobility." Why not call the nation higher? Why not call every single American to pursue their talents and dreams with greatness?

> **"Why not focus on Americans' ability to improve their economic status beyond that of the previous generation—to increase their "economic mobility"? Why not call the nation higher?"**

We already know America's real unemployment numbers, but let's tie the numbers to what having a job means for economic mobility. First, understand that upward mobility in the United States has *decreased* over the last couple of decades.

According to the American Enterprise Institute (AEI), it has "stagnated." However, AEI offers a solution. In March of 2014, AEI said:

"Having a job is the surest way out of poverty. There is an immediate need to encourage more participation in the labor force following the [2008 crash]."[15]

Catch that? The key to increasing economic mobility is to increase and incentivize work force participation. Neither the President, leaders on Capitol Hill, nor the media even mention that. Rather, they talk about more government systems. We've seen the result of systems. No thanks. Sorry, Julia.

On a broader scale, the systems—and higher taxes—that cushioned Julia's life have hurt our position on the world stage. We're less competitive. We have the highest corporate tax rate in the developed world.[16] According to the Heritage Foundation's Index of Economic Freedom, the United States ranks only "mostly free." We're not even in the top 10. Try 12th place.[17] Under President George W. Bush, we ranked fifth. Today, Hong Kong, Australia, Switzerland, Canada, and Ireland all fall ahead of United States.[18] Why? In 2015, The Heritage Foundation said:

"The regulatory burden has been mounting. Since 2009, over 150 new major regulations have been imposed at

an annual cost of more than $70 billion. As of 2014, 125
new regulations were in the pipeline."[19]

Want to start a business? Perhaps you could use flashcards to study-up on the new regulations. Well that's the hole and it's a big one. We better decide how to dig out. Understand that our deficits, national debt, and dismal unemployment numbers are not the real problem. The habits that led to those results are the problem. The habits of wasteful spending and unending government regulations are the problem.

Famed economist Milton Friedman said, "Nothing is so permanent as a temporary government program."[20] Strong point. When was the last time you read of a government program closing its doors? Friedman also said, "One of the greatest mistakes is to judge policies and programs by their intentions rather than their results."[21] Think about Julia. The intention was that the system would help her, but the results were a crushed economy—that in reality—set her back.

I'll make this simple. We can't change the results overnight, but we can change our nation's habits. Folks in Washington will only change when we the America voters have a change in heart. If we change our habits, we can inspire a change in our leaders' habits. By changing habits, we'll change the results. But remember this: as individual Americans, we cannot bring restoration to America's economy by being products of a system; but we can bring restoration by being products of our individual talents and dreams.

Own your personal economy. Make wise decisions (see Chapter Three). Tell your story. Bring to the table your talents, dreams, and innovations. Let's rid our mindset of government systems and realize that systems are like a jar. Once we're in that jar, we can only grow as big as the jar. Remember too that we are part of a robust global economy. This isn't about American companies against American companies. This isn't about one state versus another. This is about American innovative might and the pursuit of unbounded growth.

Give A Damn… Because Our Economy Craves Innovative Minds

- 5 -

Give A Damn...
Because We're Ripe For Another 9/11

Shots fired. On January 7, 2015, just before noon local time in the "City of Lights," bullets lit up the headquarters of Charlie Hebdo—a Paris based satirical newspaper. Two men wearing masks, black clothing, and bulletproof vests busted in—immediately killing a security officer and a receptionist. Then they worked their way to an 11:30 a.m. editorial meeting.[1] Their target was in front of them—the Charlie Hebdo staff.

In 2012, the same staff had published a series of satirical cartoons poking fun at Islam's prophet, Muhammad. In some of the caricatures, Muhammad was nude.[2] In 2011, Hebdo's cover featured a cartoon of the prophet saying "100 lashes if you don't die of laughter!"[3] Under Sharia law, death is the punishment for slandering Muhammad. Assumedly, the two men had come to bring that punishment. Eight staff members, including five of Charlie Hebdo's cartoonists were killed.[4] A few workers found safety on the roof and shot video of the fleeing attackers.[5] They traded fire with police officers who stood in their way.

In one instance, the men executed an officer at point blank range on a Paris sidewalk. He had been lying down with his hands up. They shot him anyway and continued in their escape.[6]

41

In total, 12 people were killed at the hands of two men screaming "Allahu Akbar!" According to a doctor that treated survivors, the gunmen separated men from women—naming specific members of the staff they intended to kill. The same doctor said the bullet wounds demonstrated precision, execution-style killings.[7]

There was no mercy or respect for Charlie Hebdo's right to freedom of expression. In the two days that followed, five more were killed in related standoffs and attacks. One of the attacks was on a Jewish grocery store.[8] Sadly enough, the 2015 attacks were not the first time the Charlie Hebdo headquarters had been targeted. In 2011, its headquarters was firebombed.[9] In the aftermath of that attack, cartoonist Stéphane Charbonnier—or "Charb," as he was known—said, "I'd rather die standing up than live on my knees."[10] What courage. He stood up for rights we often take for granted.

Following the 2015 attacks, on January 11, 3.7 million people marched across Paris. They stood in solidarity against radical Islamic terror. Forty world leaders joined the march, including Israeli prime minister, Benjamin Netanyahu, and Palestinian Authority president, Mahmoud Abbas.[11] More than enemies, the two men stood only feet from each other. Noticeably absent was President Obama, which strikes a remarkable parallel to America's handling of radical Islamic terror. Here in the United States, we may be further away, but radical Islamists harbor no respect for our rights either. Though the moment marked a flashpoint in world history, America was absent. If our approach to fighting radical Islam doesn't change, similar attacks will soon hit our shores.

Here in America, we are weak. Our leaders, President Obama included, will not call evil for evil. The President and his administration refuse to call radical Islamic terror, *radical Islamic terror*. The habit has relaxed our nation into a pre-9/11 mindset. I would argue that we're set-up for another 9/11, perhaps worse.

Despite attacks carried out by self-described, Islamic jihadist's here at home and abroad, the President never blames radical Islam—simply "radicalism." Instead, he has befriended leaders of radical Islamic groups here in America. For example, Imam Mohamed Magid is the President of the Islamic Society of North America or "ISNA."[12]

The organization was once an un-indicted co-conspirator in the Holy Land Foundation Trial—the largest terrorism financing trial in U.S. history.[13] Imam Magid has visited the White House on numerous occasions during President Obama's time in office.[14] Mr. Obama personally recorded a congratulatory video to be aired at the group's 50th national convention in 2013.[15] ISNA frequently labels critics of Islam and radical Islam as "Islamophobes." The group also maintains close, radical ties with the Muslim Brotherhood in Egypt and the Middle East.

Unlike our President and some on Capitol Hill, let's label the radicalism for what it is: *radical Islamic terror*. That bears repeating. The greatest evil of our time, which threatens our very way of life, is radical Islamic terror. Radical Islamists brought down the World Trade Center on September 11, 2001. Radical Islamists bombed the Madrid subway system on March 11, 2004.[16] Radical Islamists bombed the London subway system on July 7, 2005.[17]

In the U.S., a radical Islamist attempted to ignite and explosive device aboard a transatlantic flight on Christmas Day in 2009.[18] A radical Islamist attempted to bomb Times Square on May 1, 2010.[19] A lone-wolf radical Islamist, Army Major Nidal Hasan, killed 13 people in Texas at Fort Hood.[20] The Obama Administration called it "workplace violence."[21] Finally, radical Islamists killed 67 people at the Westgate Mall in Nairobi, Kenya in September 2013.[22] It would seem to me that the issue isn't "radicalism." The threat is "radical Islamic terror." Understanding the threat and the ideology is the key to addressing it.

So what is radical Islamic terror? What do radical Islamists desire? They want two things. First, they want to restore the "Global Islamic Caliphate"—most often described as a Muslim-led, one-world government bent on conquering the West. In other words, it is an Islamic state bent on destroying our way of life. Second, they want to establish "Sharia" law everywhere. Sharia is simply the Islamic legal system.[23]

If the world fell under a Global Islamic Caliphate, the entire world—Muslim or not—would fall under Sharia. To further understand the ideology, understand that the majority of radical Islamists believe that lying to non-Muslims for the protection of

Islam is allowed. Muslims however, are not allowed to lie to each other under Sharia law.[24] Understand that it was Sharia law that motivated the Charlie Hebdo attackers to gun down the artists who "slandered" the prophet Muhammad. Under Sharia law, there is no freedom of expression. Only death awaits those who dare step out of line.

That is the threat, but our President and his administration remain stubborn. Despite his stubbornness, we must look forward to the 2016 elections. As a country, we must understand that radical Islamic terror is the greatest evil of our time. That's because radical Islam is spreading. They control parts of Syria, Iraq, and nearly all of Yemen.[25] They control parts of Africa and have a significant presence in Europe. They have influence in Indonesia. President Ronald Reagan knew that Communism was the greatest evil of *his* time. He called it for what it was and addressed the threat. President Franklin Roosevelt knew that Nazism was the greatest evil of *his* time. He called it for what it was and addressed the threat.

> **"Under Sharia law, there is no freedom of expression. Only death awaits those who dare step out of line."**

In that vein, America is not to be a warmonger. That's unrestrained power. We should be the authority and moral leader on peace because we are the only country in the world with the strength and wherewithal to carry that message. It's impossible for the United States to be the world's police. That would bankrupt us. However, we can set the example for peace. We can influence peace and we can leverage our power where it is most effective. Evil will find no resting place if our nation inspires other nations to root it out.

We can't forget that America faces radical Islam on two fronts. The Middle East isn't the only problem. Our borders pose a major threat. We must act on both fronts. The Mexican and Canadian borders are wide open. Each provides a major opportunity for radical Islamists to come and go as they please. I'll use the southern border as an example. Cochise County, Arizona knows all too well the threat posed by drug cartels and violent, illegal immigrants. Border ranchers in that county have seen cartel members carrying AK-47s and bails of marijuana.[26]

They've also seen trails of illegals make nightly trips into the United States. Some of the ranchers have seen more. According to a July 2014 interview by TheBlaze with a U.S. Customs and Border Patrol agent—speaking on terms of anonymity—there is "no doubt" that individuals from Afghanistan and Pakistan are crossing our southern border. Further, the agent said, "We've found Korans, prayer rugs, and many other unusual items at the border that certainly raise concern."[27]

It's more disconcerting when an American-born Islamic State supporter supports the agent's claim. Christopher Cornell was captured by an undercover FBI operation in January of 2015. He had over 600 rounds of ammunition and had planned to attack the U.S. Capitol. From jail, Cornell told a Cincinnati,

Ohio reporter, "There will be many, many attacks [on America]." Further, he said:

"We're in Texas. We're in Ohio. We're in New York City. We're in Washington, DC. We're in every single state you can name, just about."[28]

We can't possibly confirm that Cornell was telling the truth. But, we can understand that both our borders provide opportunities for radical Islamists to get here easily. The fact that terrorists are likely using our borders to travel here is reason enough that we should secure them.

Understanding the threat of radical Islam and the role America should play in addressing that threat, where do we go from here? In the HBO show "The Newsroom," actor Jeff Daniels plays Will McAvoy—a respected and sometimes cranky evening news anchor. During the opening scene of the first season, McAvoy is speaking on a panel in front of college students. With regard to America's problems, he says, "The first step in solving any problem is recognizing there is one."[29]

America, forget about President Obama for a moment. Forget about Washington. The threat we face is reason enough to give a damn. The first step in addressing it is to recognize it—to call it for what it is. In the military, the first step to understanding the threat should be to understand "the enemy threat doctrine"—the lens by which radical Islamists view the world.

In this case, as terrorism expert John Guandolo would put it, "The enemy threat doctrine is Sharia (Islamic law)."

Guandolo also says, "It is what the enemy states it is fighting to impose on the world, and it is the blueprint for all they do."[30] If we don't understand what radical Islamic terrorists are fighting for, we can't understand what they're trying to accomplish or even their next move. Simply, the enemy threat doctrine is the proper starting place. If we don't start there, we're no different than President Obama, who actively ignores the true threat.

Similar to the Charlie Hebdo attackers, radical Islamic terrorists don't care about your rights. They don't care if you're a Christian, a Jew, or an atheist. If you are not Muslim, you are the enemy. They don't care about your freedom to express yourself. If you "slander" the prophet Muhammad, they seek to punish you with death. Living "across the pond" here in America doesn't insulate us. Remember, radical Islamists seek to conquer and end our way of life. They want global Islamic government and law—much like Hitler wanted Nazism to rule the world. Can't you see how radical Islamic terror is the greatest evil of our time? Even if our President cannot, we must stand united, un-intimidated, unafraid, and ultimately informed about what we face as a people.

As with everything else, we the American voters must inspire the change we wish to see. If we want our President or the person we elect in 2016 to understand the threat, we must understand the threat. We don't have to wait for radical Islamic terrorists to hit America again for us to unite as one.

Give A Damn... Because We're Ripe For Another 9/11

- 6 -

Give A Damn...
Because Our Foreign Policy Emboldens Evil

He held peace in his hands. As one commentator put it, "One man saved us from the greatest war of all. Posterity will thank God as we do now, that in our hour of desperate need, our safety was guarded by such a man..."[1] So they thought.

In 1938, German chancellor, Adolf Hitler, was tearing across Europe on his mission to create a "greater Germany."[2] He wanted to expand Germany's borders and create the world's greatest super power. Though steeped in evil, that was Hitler's vision and he was on the move. He had no respect for the borders of other nations and at the time, Germany had already taken over Austria.[3] Evil's next stop was Czechoslovakia and they knew it. The Czechoslovakian government had hoped the French and British would come to their aid if Hitler invaded. They were wrong.

British Prime Minister, Neville Chamberlain, and French Prime Minister, Édouard Daladier, had decided their countries were not ready for war. Instead, they chose to negotiate with Hitler—to negotiate and appease evil. In September of 1938, Prime Minister Chamberlain traveled to Germany twice. Chamberlain offered favorable terms, but Hitler wanted more.

He wanted the Sudetenland part of Czechoslovakia.[4] Hitler argued that the Sudetenland consisted of mostly German-speaking people.[5] At the negotiation table, Hitler wanted the Sudetenland; but in reality, he wanted more.

On September 30, 1938, Chamberlain cowered to Hitler's demands. He signed what was called the "Munich Agreement," which gave Hitler what he wanted. He got the Sudetenland and the path to more. That same day, Chamberlain flew home. In front of 10 Downing Street, the Prime Minister's official residence, Chamberlain said this while holding the "Munich Agreement":

> *"My good friends, for the second time in our history, a British Prime Minister has returned from Germany bringing peace with honor. I believe it is "peace for our time." Go home and get a nice quiet sleep."*[6]

He should have added, "You're going to need it." Chamberlain held peace in his hands. According to that commentator, "One man saved us from the greatest war of all." So they thought. The very next day, on September 31, 1938, Hitler took the Sudetenland and threatened the rest of Czechoslovakia into submission. By March 1939—less than a year later—evil broke the Munich Agreement and took the rest of Czechoslovakia.[7] The country ceased to exist and Germany's borders grew wider. Evil grew wider because Chamberlain appeased Hitler.

Emboldened by the Czechoslovakia land-grab, Hitler invaded Poland on September 1, 1939.[8] Britain and France threatened to intervene, but Hitler had seen those cards before. He wasn't worried. Two days after the invasion, Chamberlain declared war on the very nation he sought to appease.[9] World War II had begun. After eight months of bad wartime leadership, Prime Minister Chamberlain was replaced by Winston Churchill.[10]

Immediately, Churchill united Britain and brought all political parties together. On May 13, 1940, he said, "I have nothing to offer but blood, toil, tears, and sweat" and declared that Britain would never surrender.[11] He didn't appease. He led with strength and declared victory well before it happened. For the first year of Churchill's leadership, Britain resisted Germany all alone. Eventually, strength and peace defeated evil. God only knows what would have been if appeasement had continued.

For Britain, appeasement didn't work. Cowering to the motives of evil didn't work. Strength did. Strength re-established peace and put down evil. Today in the United States, appeasement is rampant. President Obama and Secretary of State, John Kerry, stood weak on holding Russia accountable when they ignored the borders of neighboring Ukraine.[12] Instead of acting against ISIS in Syria and Iraq when it mattered, they watched the Middle East catch fire. It burns even hotter today.

The President and his administration also watched Yemen fall into the hands of radical Islamic rebels.[13] China, the nation who owns more than \$1 trillion of America's national debt, often manipulates their currency. The President knows that, but has done nothing to address the problem. The constant manipulation by China costs the United States millions of jobs.[14] What's the common theme here? These are the results of unchecked, evil motives. They're the product of appeasement and a complete lack of strength—at a time when strength is needed.

Much like Hitler did ahead of World War II, Russian president, Vladimir Putin, has ignored the sovereign borders of neighboring Ukraine. As a point of history, Ukraine became part of Soviet Russia in 1922—four years after the end of World War I.[15] After Soviet Russia collapsed in 1991, Ukraine regained its independence.[16] Whether Putin actually seeks to retake all of the former Soviet territory is unclear. At a minimum, he wants Ukraine.

In February 2014, immediately following a revolution in Ukraine, Putin told a meeting of his security services chiefs that "we must start returning [the Crimean peninsula of Ukraine] to Russia."[17] It was then that the United States should have acted. Carrying the rod of peace with our allies, crippling sanctions should have been placed on Russia. If they were going to take Ukraine, Russia should have first been made to clear the hurdle of destroying their economy.

President Obama and members of Congress talked tough, but there was hardly any action. Now Congress and the President did place some sanctions on Russia, but they were minimal. So

Putin moved forward. His stated goal of "returning Crimea to Russia" was eerily similar to Hitler's goal to take the Sudetenland. Before Hitler sought to take the Sudetenland, he claimed his troops were on the border of Czechoslovakia to protect ethnic Germans.

Fast forward to 2014. In similar fashion, Putin claimed his troops were on the border of Ukraine to protect ethic Russians on the Crimean peninsula.[18] And following the Ukrainian revolution in February 2014, a referendum was put to a likely manipulated vote on the Crimean peninsula.[19] There was no "Munich Agreement," but the result was similar. Crimea would become part of "Mother Russia."

Putin's victory lap was a striking parallel to Hitler's rhetoric. In his 2014 State of the Nation address, Putin said, "Crimea is where our people live."[20] Taking Crimea wasn't enough. Even after it was over, Putin placed Russian troops on the border of Ukraine as a show of force. He later pulled them back.[21] Appeasement and weakness allowed Putin's Russia to advance.

Also under President Obama's watch, Middle East conflict has grown from a small blaze to a raging forest fire. The President has done everything but abandon Israel. As our strongest Middle East ally, Israel is surrounded by nations that wish to wipe them off the map. As mentioned in Chapter Five, radical Islamic terror is on the rise. I should note that Yemen's government, has fallen to Islamic rebels.[22] This was once a nation where President Obama touted success. In September 2014, he said:

"This strategy of taking out terrorists who threaten us, while supporting partners on the front lines, is one that we have successfully pursued in Yemen and Somalia for years ..."[23]

Though radical Islamic terror is the greatest evil of our time, the President wants Americans to believe the "Global War on Terror" is over and that al Qaeda has been "decimated." As a result, Iraq and Syria have become safe havens for the likes of ISIS. The ruthless, radical Islamists want the entire world to fall under their rule and our president refuses to take the threat seriously.

At the time of this writing, the administration is brokering a deal with Iran to prevent it from developing a nuclear weapon. Iran is one of the world's largest state sponsors of terrorism.[24] Since the 1970s, the country has desired to wipe Israel off the map. Secretary of State, John Kerry, was put in charge of the negotiations. While the negotiations were ongoing, Iran's supreme leader, Ayatollah Khamenei responded to a crowd chanting, "Death to America." He said, "Of course, yes, death to America..."[25]

On April 2, 2015, President Obama announced from the White House Rose Garden that the "framework" for a deal had been reached. He said current sanctions on Iran would be phased out.[26] But days after Obama's announcement, Iranian president, Hassan Rouhani, said his country would *not* sign a nuke deal until *all* sanctions were lifted.[27] One word could be used to describe Iran: deceit. President Obama will have to decide whether to channel his best Chamberlain or Churchill. When the deal is done, perhaps, he'll hold "peace" in his hands.

Understand this, these are the results of over six years of appeasement and cowering to evil. Some on the left would say the results are mischaracterized; and so would some on the right. Forget right and left. Forget Republican or Democrat. Forget labels. Prime Minister Chamberlain and his successor, Winston Churchill were members of the same political party. Ideology wasn't the issue.

Chamberlain represented appeasement. Churchill represented strength. One left the evil of Adolf Hitler unchecked. The other achieved peace and placed Hitler on the ash heap of history. Based on his characteristics and actions as a leader, President Obama represents appeasement. This attitude towards America's foreign policy has left Russia unchecked, Iran unchecked, and ISIS unchecked. When evil motives go unchecked, the results of evil go forth unrestrained.

The 2016 Presidential Election must mark a shift from President Obama's Chamberlain-style appeasement to Churchill's strength. The nations of the world—especially those who seek to do evil—must understand that America will command a position of strength. We cannot tolerate countries disrespecting the borders of their neighbors as Russia has in Ukraine. We cannot tolerate countries who manipulate currencies to obtain unfair, international trading power.

We cannot tolerate the spread of radical Islamic terror—the greatest evil of our time. And while we cannot police the world without first bankrupting ourselves, we can use the rod of peace to protect our people at home and influence peace abroad. That is the responsibility of our nation—to carry the torch of liberty and bear rod of peace. America is the only nation with the strength and wherewithal to own that responsibility.

Understand that our next President must command strength on day one—from the moment he or she completes the oath of office. That strength will set the tone, command respect, and hopefully, set appeasement aside for good. We must embolden our allies to join us in rooting out evil. Our strength will be supported by an effectively communicated vision—that America will not the police the world, but will leverage its power for peace and stability. The message of that vision should allow every American to understand and hold it in the palm of their hand.

Examine history for yourself and realize that if we appease our enemies, evil will spread and America's existence in the next century will become questionable. Remember, if you don't see strength in America's leaders, you must inspire it. You must become strong, carry the torch of liberty, and help bear the rod of peace.

- 7 -

Give A Damn...
Because Government Wants To Be Your Doctor

John and Sarah love their home in northern Virginia. They have two beautiful children. Jennifer is 15 and finishing up high school. She hits the A-B honor roll every year and runs track. Jack is 18 and heading off to college to study engineering. To take care of their children, John and Sarah have worked hard and done well. Sarah has been a nurse for more than a decade. John has been in pharmaceutical sales for about the same. But with Jack heading off to college and Jennifer just three years behind, money is tight.

They had prepared and saved some money for their children's education, but it wasn't enough. Rapidly rising tuition costs made it hard to stay on track. To avoid taking out loans, they'll pay out of pocket to shore up what college savings won't cover. Education aside, John and Sarah are still trying to recover from the 2008 market crash—when the value of their home dropped nearly $100,000 dollars. In 2007, they had started saving for retirement, but 2008 wiped out most of their gains. They're still trying to catch-up. Needless to say, there isn't much cash left over at the end of the month.

What about health insurance? The pharmaceutical company that John works for pays for his family's healthcare coverage. Now John's company requires him to contribute some of his income toward the cost of the insurance plan. The contribution is reasonable and is automatically deducted from his paychecks. The hospital where Sarah works also offers healthcare coverage, but Sarah chooses to stay on her husband's plan. For them and their kids, visits to the doctor have always been affordable— typically a $15 co-pay. The same has been true for prescription drugs.

But if he's honest, John is worried. His company is already talking about the changes coming from the Affordable Care Act or "Obamacare," as it's known. Life is about to get more expensive. Insurance premiums are going up and members of the company's sales staff, like John, will be contributing *more* of their paycheck towards health insurance. But wait, things are already tight.

How will they afford it? What about Jack's college tuition? What's going to happen when both of the kids are in college? Of more concern, there are rumors that the company has considered cutting the sales staff from full to part-time—less than 30 hours per week. That way, under Obamacare, the company isn't even required to provide health insurance. Seriously? Will John have to get another job? Will he have to pay for health insurance out of pocket? It's certainly possible.

So what makes this law "affordable?" And why are these changes just now going into effect—right after President

Obama leaves office and the 2016 election is over? Good question. If the 2010 numbers compiled by CNN are true, there will be 170 million Americans asking the same question when the changes rollout. Now John and Sarah aren't a real family, but that situation is real for millions of Americans. Obamacare will have a very real impact. Will it be a positive one? Likely not.

Before President Obama took office on January 20, 2009, healthcare in America was in a death spiral towards brokenness and bankruptcy. Some would argue it still is. After President Obama took office, the Affordable Care Act was priority number one. He and the Democrats controlled the White House and both houses of Congress. It was the perfect time to change the face of American healthcare forever.

According to them, the situation was dire. Nearly 50 million Americans were uninsured—roughly 16 percent of the total population.[1] "We've got to do something!" they said. What was their solution? Change the *entire* system instead of simply addressing rising healthcare costs and the 50 million uninsured. Over the next year, Congressional Democrats put together a 2,700-page bill for the President to sign on March 23, 2010.[2] Off the top, the new law expanded access to healthcare, but did nothing meaningful to address rising costs.

Now based upon your own homework, you can decide how you feel about Obamacare. Some would argue that the following are positive achievements of the law. From a pure access-to-healthcare standpoint, some would argue the bill works well. The law created a system by which 50 million uninsured individuals could become insured. For young people, the law allows them to stay on their parents' health insurance till age 26.[3] The law also requires health insurance companies to offer free preventative care. For many, *this* is a big positive: you can't be denied healthcare coverage because of a pre-existing condition. Finally, if you can't afford health insurance, the federal government will help you buy it.[4]

Positives aside, what makes law work? Every single American is required to buy health insurance—like it or not. Now whether you consider this a positive depends on how much you like your personal liberty. There are two components to the law's requirement: the individual mandate and the employer mandate.

If you, as an individual, are self-employed or unemployed, you're required to buy health insurance. If you don't, the IRS will charge you a penalty come tax season.[5] If you're employed by a company like John or Sarah, your employer is required to provide health insurance if you work "full-time." If your company doesn't, the IRS will charge the company a penalty come tax season. Under the law, full time means more than 30 hours per week, not the traditional 40 hours.[6] The first requirement is called the "individual mandate" and the second is called the "employer mandate."

The individual mandate is already in effect. The effects of the employer mandate won't be felt till President Obama leaves office and the 2016 elections are over. Wonder why. Perhaps there will be a lot of ticked off Johns and Sarahs to go around and they would take out their frustrations on Democrats. Remember, not a single House Republican voted for Obamacare.[7]

Now that America's national debt has passed $18 trillion, how much will Obamacare cost going forward? According to The Wall Street Journal, the cost to build Healthcare.gov alone cost $840 million.[8] Most of the cost was the result of a horrendous rollout. According to ObamacareFacts.com, Obamacare related spending is expected to rise at an unsustainable rate—which will increase America's deficit spending.[9] That means America will continue to spend more than it takes in. Oh, in case you're wondering, the law is designed to make younger, healthier people pay for older, sicker people.[10] What an incentive! Stay young and healthy so you can pay *more*!

That aside, my greatest concern about Obamacare is that it increased access and lowered the *quality* of care for many. It increased access for those who didn't have it, but lowered the quality for folks like John and Sarah. Many individuals under similar circumstances have seen an increase in the cost of their healthcare, but found out that their plan no longer covers their favorite doctors.

As an example, when President Obama was selling the law to we the American voter, he said, "If you like the plan you have, you can keep it. If you like the doctor you have, you can keep your doctor, too." After the law was passed, one of the chief architects of Obamacare, Dr. Ezekiel Emanuel, had something different to say. Appearing on Fox News Sunday in December 2013, he said, "If you want to pay [*more*] for an insurance company that covers your doctor, you can do that."[11]

Worse than a broken promise, while Democrats went on and on about the rising costs of healthcare before the bill passed, the actual law barely addressed hospital and prescription drug costs. Hospital and drug costs continue to skyrocket.[12] And while Democrats called the insurance website a "Marketplace"— evoking thoughts of competition and lower prices—the law did not allow insurance companies to compete across state lines. That's not good news for those who buy their own health insurance.

> **"Given the scope of the law, the relationship is quickly becoming a three party relationship: doctor, government, and patient."**

If you are a Virginia resident, you must buy Virginia-based health insurance. If you're a Florida resident, you must buy Florida-based health insurance. As a buyer, your choices are narrowed to only the companies doing business in the state you live. That's like allowing you to attend college, but only in the state you live. Your choices would be fewer and likely more expensive. In a basic economic sense, more choices equal lower prices. Less choice equals higher prices. In the healthcare market, insurance premiums will likely be lower when more insurance companies are competing for your business. If companies were allowed to compete across state lines, that would be possible.

I can't possibly address all the problems with Obamacare. However, I do believe the supporters of the law had a larger goal in mind. For liberty lovers, it's not a good one. For those who like choice, it's not a good one. Before Obamacare, the relationship you had with your doctor was simple. It was a two party relationship: doctor and patient. You did what your doctor thought was best. Every once and a while, you got a second opinion. Given the scope of the law, the relationship is quickly becoming a three party relationship: doctor, government, and patient. Now, before giving you advice, your doctor must navigate both the law and it's regulations to ensure compliance.

Remember this: President Obama, Dr. Ezekiel Emanuel, and House minority leader, Nancy Pelosi (D-CA), truly want a complete, government-run healthcare system—sort of like the VA. Though it sounds great, ask Suzanne Chase from Chapter 2 about her experience. Despite passing Obamacare in 2009 (which doesn't include a government-run option), government-run healthcare is still the desire.

While running for president in 2008, then-Senator Obama was speaking at an AFL-CIO conference and said, "A universal healthcare plan, that's what I'd like to see. But as all of you know, we may not get there immediately." Both Dr. Emanuel and Leader Pelosi have made similar statements. That's the real endgame behind Obamacare. It was meant to move the ball down the field. Under the *real* end game, the John and Sarahs of the world wouldn't get a choice of doctors; they would get what they get. In the same AFL-CIO speech, the President said his desire would be a system that says, "Everybody in. Nobody out."[13] What do you think of those choices? Sound like the America of choice and opportunity you once knew?

Understand that your healthcare is about one thing. You. It's not about insurance companies. It's not about government. It's about you, your health, and your life. As for your healthcare, the only individuals at the table should be you and your doctor. Government shouldn't have a seat at the table. Government officials should not be allowed to bring ideas that are intended for the masses into the discussion over your personal health.

There's nothing wrong with increasing access to healthcare for those who truly can't afford it. However, quality of care for those who have health insurance shouldn't suffer in the effort to provide the access. If the concern was truly about uninsured individuals, Democrats could have simply covered the uninsured for far less than the cost of Obamacare.

They could have increased competition among hospitals, drug companies, and insurance companies for far less than the cost of Obamacare. But what happened in 2009 wasn't about decreasing costs or increasing quality and competition. It was about getting the ball down the field for a touchdown—where the end zone is painted with words "Government-Run Healthcare." Before Obamacare passed, Minority Leader Pelosi once remarked that insurance companies would be "crying out" for a government-run option.[14]

In 2016, don't be distracted by the mounds of details surrounding Obamacare. It's true, America's healthcare system is still a mess. The new law made it worse. You'll see that play out when the "Employer Mandate" kicks in after the 2016 elections are over. Perhaps you'll find yourself feeling like John and Sarah. Understand that this is about you, the American individual. Like you, I desire a solution that brings down the costs of healthcare. I desire a solution that gives me more choice over my health insurance. I desire a solution that increases access for those who truly can't afford it, but I don't desire a solution that lowers quality of care for all.

> **"Understand that your healthcare is about one thing. You. It's not about insurance companies. It's not about government. It's about you, your health, and your life."**

Who knows what's best for you—your doctor or the federal government? Washington can barely run the IRS and the VA. Do you want unelected officials making your healthcare decisions? Unless we inspire a change, unless we arm ourselves with wisdom, our government will become more involved in our healthcare. Healthcare will become "everybody in, nobody out." As for me and my healthcare, Washington can stay the hell out.

Give A Damn... Because Government Wants To Be Your Doctor

- 8 -

Give A Damn...
Because Student Debt Stalls The American Dream

He was the ideal candidate with the necessary credentials. In 2012, he was 18 years old and an all-American guy. He was the captain of his varsity basketball and football teams. He was an Eagle Scout and the thread of entrepreneurship was woven on his heart.[1] Charlie Kirk went after opportunities and always bucked the status quo.

In his words, he "always gravitated towards something different." When it came time for college, his eyes were set on the United States Military Academy at West Point. He certainly had the résumé and the required Congressional nomination. But despite his track record of achievement and leadership, he was denied acceptance. It was the setback that set him up for success.

While finishing out high school, he considered other colleges. The application and student loan process quickly frustrated him—as the federal government had taken over the student loan business in 2009.[2] Though he was passionate about history and economics, he wasn't sure college was the best investment at the time. After all, tuition prices were insane and the economy was in bad shape. At the same time, he was plugging in to conservative politics. Becoming more involved, he noticed that the liberal left often visited his high school. Kirk couldn't help but notice that conservatives weren't fighting for his generation. Between that and the student loan process, he was angry. But anger turned to opportunity and vision. Seeing that no one would fight for his generation, he started Turning Point USA—a student movement for free markets and limited government. He also took a year off between high school and his first year at The King's College in New York.

By the way, at the time of this writing, he's only 21 years old. Kirk's West Point setback forced him to rethink his approach to college. It forced him to own his personal economy and look for opportunities. What felt like a failure catapulted him towards restoration, growth, and impact. On June 5, 2012, Turning Point USA started small. Today, the organization has a presence on 800 college campuses nationwide.[3] Kirk's story should make all of us think about college differently. Today, simply attending college doesn't mean we're owed a job in our field of study.

America's job market has changed. America's slow economy and the changing global economy has reduced the number of jobs available here at home. Despite that reduction, colleges are charging record tuition rates and turning out more graduates.[4] As a result, young Americans have large amounts of student debt and are overeducated for the jobs they have—if they have one at all. They're putting off marriage, starting families later, and saying no to buying a home. Those life chapters are simply unaffordable.[5] According to the Wall Street Journal:

"New households are forming at less than 40% of the normal rate. Young adults are living with their parents at much higher rates than before the Great Recession."[6]

A slow economy and student debt has truly stalled the American Dream. How did this happen? Remember President Obama's first term priority? It was healthcare. Remember the infamous debate over the 2,700-page bill? That's when the stall began. Now I'm sure you thinking, "Wait, what? It did?" You're not alone. The majority of Americans didn't notice because of the loud healthcare debate. In fact, the student loan takeover was slipped inside of the healthcare bill.[7] What's funny is the student loan take over—in many ways—mirrors the healthcare overhaul. Basically, both laws expanded access and did nothing to address rising costs—which is nothing short of pure idiocy. The student loan business needed reform, but not a complete takeover. True reform would have called for increased competition, reduced costs, and lower tuition. What actually happened didn't address any of those issues.

After the reform, the federal government began giving away student loans like candy and students took them. Who took on the risk? The students and the federal government did. What about the colleges and institutions? Nothing. No risk. They get the cash up front. Regardless of student performance or job placement, they still get the cash. There's no incentive to cut costs, lower tuition, compete for students' business, or exceed expectations. In fact, tuition rates continue to skyrocket.

The increase in tuition far outpaces inflation.[8] Under this model, there's been a massive increase in student debt since 2009. There are over $1 trillion in outstanding student loans.[9] Further, more than 10 percent of those loans are in default.[10] What's worse? According to Kirk, only about 42 percent of college students ever graduate. What's even worse? The average student loan debt per person (at the time of this writing) is over $30,000.[11]

Now our knee-jerk reaction is to blame the colleges. And while it may be fun to give them a hard time, they've done what the federal government allowed them to do. It's a government-controlled system with government-controlled interest rates. And given the level of outstanding student debt, it's a government created crisis. It's a crisis pulling the reigns on the American Dream. All of this begs the question, "Will there be a bailout?" Will Congress wipe it all away and add to the national debt? In my mind, the answer is no.

Ultimately, the student loan disaster train is going to stop one of two ways. Either we can wait till the situation blows up or Congress can stabilize the problem by returning the student loan business to the private sector. As Washington goes, the first is the likely outcome. But know that the issue isn't limited to the failure of one political party over the other. Both Republicans and Democrats are responsible for the "solution" that created the current crisis. The 2009 student loan takeover was moronic, asinine, and every synonym in between. The takeover represented a complete misunderstanding of how markets and tuition prices actually work.

It's time to end this disaster and from Kirk's perspective, higher education should be returned to the private sector. I agree with him. If so, tuition prices would decrease and colleges would be forced to compete for students' business. They would have to take on some risk and focus on graduation rates and job placement. "If schools aren't hitting certain metrics, they shouldn't be in business," said Kirk. On the individual level, students would be forced to think critically whether college is their best option. They would expect less from government and more from colleges.

Kirk believes that the private sector approach would fix our nation's student debt problem. He thinks it would right the ship as quickly as four years and that tuition would fall "30 to 40 percent." Admittedly, some schools would close. Programs that don't produce jobs would disappear. Competition would increase among surviving schools. Further, the typical four-year approach would come into question.

Of course, there will always be students who are qualified—mentally—for higher education, but will never be able to afford it. If the federal government is the mechanism to help them, fine. But before we talk about expanding ways to do that, we should keep our focus on decreasing tuition prices. Now if our country's higher education system needs a real overhaul, why does Washington keep the status quo? Personally, I think it's in their DNA.

Kirk believes our leaders are holding out because this is "all about political control on the right and left. This is about keeping control over throngs of students. It looks more like politicians choosing against wisdom for political leverage over a large voting block."

It's time to buck the status quo. Remember, simply going to college does not mean you'll come out with a job. We've got to think deeper than that and analyze what we want to do. We have to ask what we're passionate about and why. And ultimately, we have to ask ourselves whether we'll see a return on our investment. Eventually, the current circumstances will force every American student to think critically about their pursuit of higher education. It will force them to examine college like an investor examines a company. It will force them to own their personal economy like Charlie Kirk did at 18 years old.

> **"This is a government created crisis. Government is bankrupting America's education and the American dream. This madness can stop."**

This is a government created crisis. Government is bankrupting America's education and the American dream. This madness can stop. Though we can lay blame on our leadership in Washington, we must also blame ourselves for not demanding better. We've watched tuition prices and student loans debt rise rapidly, but what have we done? Nothing. Have we made ourselves heard? Have we banded together as we the American voters—the largest grass roots organization in the United States? No. If not, then *why* not?

As with everything America will face in the 2016 elections, we must change on the individual, heart level if we're to inspire change in Washington. The student loan status quo doesn't define America's future.

Give A Damn... Because Student Debt Stalls The American Dream

- 9 -

Give A Damn...
Because Our Phones Are Tapped

He was frustrated. Kirk Wiebe had devoted his entire life to protecting Americans. Now, the agency he worked for was turning against them. As a communications intelligence expert at the National Security Agency (NSA), much of Wiebe's career was spent managing and building systems to stop the bad guys—from enemy nations to terrorists. He was granted security clearance back in 1964; and later in his career, he received the Meritorious Civilian Service Award. It's the NSA's second highest honor.[1]

But everyday work and awards aside, Wiebe knew that his primary responsibility was to "support and defend the Constitution of the United States against all enemies, foreign and domestic..."[2] He knew that despite his intelligence gathering role, he was to protect Americans' privacy. He was to honor the Fourth Amendment. On that, there would be no compromise.

If there was anyone who had known the purpose and history of the NSA, it was Wiebe. He knew why the NSA was created in 1952. World War II had come to a close in 1945 when President Harry Truman dropped two atomic bombs on Japan.

Though the war was over, the United States had learned a lesson. The use of coded communications by the enemies had shown President Truman that the United States needed a better intelligence game. The World War II systems were not sufficient. On October 24, 1952, Truman ordered the creation of the NSA. Its purpose was to:

"[P]rovide an effective, unified organization and control of the communications intelligence activities of the United States conducted against foreign governments."[3]

Wiebe understood the NSA's purpose. The agency was to collect intel on foreign enemies and not American citizens. But today, the battlefield is more complicated. We live in the age of terrorism. Our conflicts aren't simply with "foreign governments." Those who wish to kill us are right here on American soil. Just like us, they use iPhones, Twitter, Gmail, YouTube, and more. In many ways, they blend in. The men who killed nearly 3,000 people on September 11, 2001 were right here in America.

After 9/11, how would the NSA provide security for Americans and protect their privacy? Wiebe knew. He knew before 9/11. He and his colleague William Binney had helped develop a system called "Thinthread."[4] It could gather intelligence on terrorists and enemies—abroad and here at home. But because that involved gathering information on

Americans, Binney and Wiebe designed a feature that would mask the identity of who the information came from. A warrant would be required to go further.

A version of Thinthread was ready to go nine months before the 9/11 attacks.[5] Unlike other big government projects, its initial development had only cost $3 million.[6] According to Wiebe, Thinthread wouldn't have missed the communications that led to 9/11. The NSA never implemented it. In 2000, the agency instead chose "Trailblazer"—an undeveloped system that never worked, spent billions, and was later cancelled in 2006.[7]

Frustrated, Weibe and Binney went to Congress in 2000 to blow the whistle on the irresponsible project. They were demoted. But after 9/11, the NSA had to act fast to cover the nation's vulnerabilities. The agency chose a program called "Stellar Wind." It was based on Thinthread, but lacked the privacy protections for American citizens. Fourth amendment be damned. The NSA was spying on Americans. The NSA was collecting and storing Americans' phone and email data. This went well beyond Truman's idea.

It was then that Wiebe recognized the massive Constitutional breach, but whistle blowing had gotten him nowhere. He took retirement from the NSA one month after 9/11. No longer at the agency, Wiebe, Benny, and congressional staffer, Diane Roark, tried to expose the Constitutional violation in 2002. They filed a complaint with the Inspector General's office in Department of

Defense. The complaint resulted in a report that confirmed the breach.[8]

Finally, a 2005 New York Times story publicly exposed what Wiebe had already known; and so did Edward Snowden in 2013. The NSA was gathering information on American citizens without a warrant.[9] Because of the New York Times article, the FBI raided the homes of every named person on the Inspector General's complaint—including the homes of Wiebe, Benny, and Roark. According to Wiebe, it was an act of intimidation. Why? None of them were ever charged with a crime.[10] That was the price of whistleblowing. That was the price of supporting and defending the Constitution.

Where are we today? To fully understand the state of our privacy, we first have to understand the right. In plain English, the Fourth Amendment provides that, generally, government cannot search or seize you, your house, your papers, or your belongings without a warrant supported by probable cause. Also, the warrant must state with specificity the place to be searched and the person or items to be taken.[11] Broad, "everything but the kitchen sink warrants" are not allowed. Now the great thing about the Fourth Amendment is that it knows no technological boundaries. "Persons, houses, papers, and effects" seems to cover most everything—including your technology.

However, know that there are some instances when a police officer doesn't need a warrant to search or arrest you. For example, an officer doesn't need warrant if you commit a felony in front of him. Also, if your car is towed or impounded, the intake officer doesn't need a warrant to "inventory" the items in your car.[12] If the officer finds drugs during the inventory, so be it.

In the case of your phone calls, emails, and other communications however, law enforcement must have a warrant to monitor them. According to Wiebe, the Department of Defense Inspector General, and the New York Times, the NSA needed warrants for what the agency was doing. That hardly ever happened. If the NSA did get a warrant, it was through a secret court where the records are not open to the public. It's called the Foreign Intelligence Surveillance Court (FISA Court).

So when did this clear violation of the Fourth Amendment begin? How did it work? One month after 9/11, President George W. Bush secretly authorized the NSA to track terrorists by monitoring Americans' communications without a warrant. He did so despite a 1978 law requiring a warrant for all domestic surveillance.[13] The result? The NSA started collecting massive amounts of your phone calls, emails, and other communications. That's not opinion. It's fact. A FISA Court order, obtained by The Guardian's Glenn Greenwald, confirms that Verizon was required to give the NSA all phone data on an "ongoing, daily basis." That included all U.S. and international phone data. This was bulk collection of Americans' phone records.[14]

Now officials backpedaled and said the NSA was only collecting the "metadata" of those calls, not the content. Metadata is data that describes other data. For phone calls, metadata is information that describes when a call took place, who the participants were, and where they were located.[15] Harmless, right? Who cares if they know where I am or who I'm talking to? They didn't hear what I said. According to the Obama Administration, collecting metadata isn't a violation of Americans' privacy rights under the Fourth Amendment. In 2013, President Obama said:

> *"By sifting through this so-called metadata, [the NSA] may identify potential leads with respect to folks who might engage in terrorism." He added that "you can't have 100 percent security and then also have 100 percent privacy and zero inconvenience."*[16]

Kirk Wiebe thinks otherwise. In an interview with PBS FRONTLINE, he said:

> *"NSA's claim that all metadata in the world does not constitute a violation of privacy is a lie, an unequivocal lie. Metadata reveals more about what you're doing ... and ... your patterns of behavior."*[17]

But the NSA loves metadata—terabytes and terabytes of metadata. In fact, the agency gave metadata a home in 2013 near Bluffdale, Utah. It cost nearly $2 billion to build, stretches more than 1 million square feet, and houses "all forms of communication."[18] Sounds like "this so-called metadata" is awfully important. Some officials would say the NSA's collection tactics have made America safer. Some would disagree. Some would say that Americans must sacrifice their privacy in the name of security. Wiebe and Binney would say otherwise. After all, they had developed a data collection system that would have protected the privacy of American citizens.

Regardless of what anyone would say, this is the age of terrorism, Middle East conflict, and cyber warfare. That means our government must fight on all fronts, cyberspace included. It must use edgy, technological methods to find and root out evil. We must know and understand that. As for managing the relationship between our security and privacy, we must gather the facts and approach it with wisdom.

Twenty-first century warfare requires innovative, visionary ways to both "support and defend" our rights and provide for our security. We can't ignore that terrorists use peaceful communication methods for purely evil purposes. Those responsible for our security must sift through communications of harmless Americans and radical Islamic terrorists alike.

Now the leaders and bureaucrats of today feel as President Obama does. Your security comes at the cost of your privacy. Our country's security measures reflect that theme. Perhaps you can understand their position. No President or agency wants

America to get attacked on their watch. They don't want blood on their hands. That's fair, but we cannot forget about our Fourth Amendment privacy rights. Once diluted, it is hard to return our rights back to their full concentration and effect.

Attempts to do so would be like returning a glass of wine back to its original flavor after a cup of water was added. That would be near impossible. Right now, the NSA has the ability to touch all of your phone and internet activities. To what extent, I'm not sure we'll ever know. For national security reasons, the process is shrouded in secrecy and classified protections. While our government's massive increase in security after 9/11 was understandable, perhaps there is a better solution.

> **"We can't ignore that terrorists use peaceful communication methods for purely evil purposes."**

The best solution to our national security must consider our Constitutionally guaranteed right to privacy. The right is non-negotiable. It is not one that government can give and take away. It is "unalienable." Now some would say, "I would gladly give up my privacy for my security. I have nothing to hide. Look at my stuff all you want." Though that statement may seem reasonable, it ignores the principle.

We are entitled to be secure in our "persons, houses, papers, and effects." The ideal solution for America's security will collect enough communications intelligence necessary to stop evil, but will also protect our privacy. We *can* have both. We must demand both. Perhaps Kirk Wiebe, William Binney, and their work on project Thinthread demonstrates that you and I can have both. We can have privacy and security. If we can't have it perfectly, our Constitution demands we strive for it.

Remember, by the very oath they swear, our leaders and national security officials promise to "support and defend the Constitution of the United States...." That takes priority over their responsibility to provide for our nation's security. Similar to our leaders' responsibility, we must hold our right to privacy in high regard. It isn't enough to hope that Washington will do it for us. As I said, rights taken away don't often return. We need a President and national security leadership that respects our rights. That necessary shift will require a principled, conscience decision on their part. We need patriots that cherish liberty, not disconnected bureaucrats. We the American voters must cherish liberty as well. Finally, we need a path for patriots like Kirk Wiebe to blow the whistle when leaders betray our trust.

Right now, if our government and the NSA aren't violating the Fourth Amendment, they're too close for comfort. If we're going to change that, a grassroots liberty revival will be necessary. A movement that simply carries flags down the National Mall won't be enough. A heart change is required. You have to care. Your privacy matters. Let no one tell you that your security must be paid for in the currency of your personal liberty.

Give A Damn... Because Our Phones Are Tapped

- 10 -

Give A Damn...
Because Guns Don't Have Trigger Fingers

Crouched down, he was uncomfortable behind the wheel well of a truck. That campus parking garage was cold and gray that night. But for him, it was worth the wait. Opportunity was headed his way. And if anything went awry, he had a gun. Everything should go as planned. She'd soon be out from a late night exam and would likely be alone. There would be no witnesses and his escape would be an easy one. The wait would soon be over.

Eventually, he heard voices, footsteps, and the friendly banter between classmates who had just finished an exam. Wait. Was she alone? He had hoped she would be. Would her friends walk her to her car? She was the only one parked on that level. He had been sure of it. Was it time to back out? What about that desire he wanted to satisfy? Would he have to use the gun? He had to be mentally ready to take that step.

At last, they were saying good night. "Have a good week!" he heard. She was now alone and headed his way. He knew ahead of time that she might check around her car. That's why he hid behind the truck. She wouldn't see him coming and was getting closer. His moment had come. Right after she passed by, he stepped up and grabbed her from behind—just as planned. How things went from here determined everything. To get his way—to satisfy that desire—he had to keep her quiet. He forced her to the ground and took out the gun. Placing it on her temple, he clicked off the safety and told her not to say anything.

Finally, he could rape her. Everything had gone as planned. He met no resistance and ironically enough, the police cars for campus safety were parked just 50 feet away. Even she noticed them. The office was closed. Nobody would stop him, not even her—certainly not Amanda Collins. She was perfectly defenseless. When he was done, he pointed the gun at her head one last time. "I like your skirt. It makes you look nice," he said. "Stay here until I'm gone." He walked off.[1] Months later, he'd rape and strangle to death Brianna Denison.[2]

Fortunately, Amanda lived, but her attacker was evil and could have been stopped. There's no denying it. From start to finish in that cold parking garage, he got what he wanted. In control, he was the evil behind the gun. He was the trigger finger that gave life to the threat—not the gun. It was him. He had left Amanda's life "hanging in the thread of a trigger pull."

How different that night could have been. What if Amanda had been able to put the force of good behind *her* gun? Because she was a law-abiding citizen, she left her gun at home. Despite having a concealed handgun permit, the law said she couldn't carry it on campus. She was in a "Gun Free Zone." But what if she had been in control? What if her trigger finger had given life to stopping a threat and the later rape and murder of another? If you read Amanda's story, she'd tell you that there was a distinct moment in which she could have stopped her attack. But she was helpless. As Amanda would put it, she and Brianna were "legislated into being a victim[s]."[3]

Considering Amanda's situation and the murder of Brianna, did you know that police officers have no binding, legal duty to protect you? For example, if officers had shown up on the scene of Amanda's rape while it was going on, they could have chosen to do nothing. They could have watched her attacker pull the trigger and there would be no punishment. Also, Amanda's family would be unable to sue the police department. Why? Because in 1981, the Supreme Court of the United States said that government has no duty to provide police protection to any *particular*, individual citizen. A police officer's duty is only to the community as a whole.[4] Did you know that?

Crayle Vanest didn't, but she does now. She's the Assistant Director of Development at Students for Concealed Carry on Campus (SCCC). It is a non-partisan organization of more than 40,000 students, professors, and others who believe that concealed handgun permit holders should be allowed to protect themselves on college campuses. Crayle embraces her Second Amendment right to keep and bear arms. She believes that her right "shall not be infringed," as the amendment says. She also believes that the Second Amendment preserves and secures the rest of the Bill of Rights. To her, the Second Amendment is the backstop for when tyranny knocks at the door. Because when government takes away guns, they're in the business of people control—not gun control. I agree with her.

But more than that, Crayle never thought her right was about hunting or "gun culture." It was about liberty, personal safety, and being aware of the threats we face. Given that police only have a duty to protect the community as a whole, she wanted to be her own first responder. She wanted to personally oversee her safety and equip others to do the same. Can you blame her?

As Crayle got more involved with SCCC, she heard countless stories of violence in "Gun Free Zones"—stories like Amanda's attack and the Virginia Tech massacre. Those stories upset her and honed her desire to equip others. It wasn't simply about owning guns. For her and SCCC, it became about keeping people safe—not just the community, but individuals too. It was about showing individuals that firearms are merely a tool—and that good can overcome evil when good trigger fingers put a stop to evil trigger fingers.

In that vein, today's mass shootings and violent crimes don't seem to shock us as a nation. We've come to expect them and we're quick to blame the inanimate gun over blaming the real problem. The problem is not the gun. The problem is evil. The problem is when evil trigger fingers put evil purposes behind the sights of a gun. The problem is leaving people vulnerable in places like college campuses and movie theaters—places that are wide open to the ills of society. Arguably, our leaders have created these "Gun Free" death traps by consistently ignoring the fact that criminals don't obey gun laws.

Let's talk about some of our most infamous "Gun Free Zones." One, 13 killed at Columbine High School in a Gun Free Zone.[5] Two, 32 killed at Virginia Tech in a Gun Free Zone.[6] Three, 6 killed at Northern Illinois University (NIU) in a Gun Free Zone.[7] Four, 20 children and 6 adults killed at Sandy Hook Elementary School in a Gun Free Zone.[8] Five, 12 killed at a Century movie theater in Aurora, Colorado in a Gun Free Zone.[9] Six, 12 killed at the Washington Navy Yard in a Gun Free Zone.[10] Shall I continue?

If criminals obeyed gun laws, "Gun Free Zones" would actually be "Gun Free." These zones are some of the most dangerous places in America. Within them, nothing will stop those who wish to do evil—except for police officers that have no binding duty to protect an individual. This very idea has created a society where mass shootings are next to normal.

So what's the solution and how do we get there? What would it take to reduce the occurrence of mass shootings and violent crime? First, let's acknowledge the common ground. Those on the left, right, and in between generally want safety for the American people. The question isn't about the goal. It's about how we get there. First, we must blame evil for violence and mass shootings. Second, it's clear that "Gun Free Zones" must be done away with. While "Gun Free" sounds nice, the tangible result is deadly.

As with most live shooting situations, police will often establish a perimeter and then close in on the attacker. In fact, that is exactly what happened at NIU. Within the five minutes between the first 911 call and the shooter being reported dead, the police established a perimeter around the building and worked their way inward. It took too long. The shooter was still able to kill five innocent people and turn the gun on himself.

Some believe that even a quick response time by police is not enough to protect those inside a classroom from an initial threat. In other words, students and teachers alike must be equipped to be their own first responders. Imminent threats of deadly force must be met with immediate and returned deadly force. That is the quickest and simplest way to reduce casualties.

To accomplish that, we must change the way we think about guns and our personal safety. We can do this through awareness, exposure, and education. We must be aware of our surroundings and circumstances by remaining vigilant. We must expose ourselves to firearms in a way that removes fear and teaches safety. Contrary to what some would have you believe, firearms don't spontaneously "go off." One of my firearms instructors once put it this way:

"I could lay my loaded firearm on this table, stare at it, pray over it, and send smoke signals to it, but it's not going to fire. Remember, guns require trigger fingers."

In addition to healthy, responsible exposure, we must educate ourselves on how firearms actually work—so that we can handle them properly. We must educate ourselves on how to effectively use firearms so that good may overcome evil. We must educate ourselves on liberty. As Crayle would say, "You can't have liberty if you can't protect your life." This responsibility of awareness, exposure, and education is an individual one. By individually changing how we think about firearms, we can change how society thinks about firearms. By changing society, we can prove that evil is the real problem—not firearms. Further, we can inspire a nation to personally oversee its liberty.

Of course, if you don't like that solution, you can try Virginia Tech's post-massacre solution:

> "... *Listen empathetically by really paying attention to what the [shooter] is saying; ask the [shooter] to leave the area and come back when they feel calmer; do not physically touch [the shooter], or try to force them to leave; move away from any object, such as scissors or heavy object that could be used as a weapon; calmly ask the [shooter] to place any weapons in a neutral location while you continue to talk to them.*"[11]

When asked about that very language in Virginia Tech's "Workplace Violence" handbook, Crayle Vanest said, "That sounds like a really good way to die." You can make your own determination.

In the time since her attack in 2007, Amanda Collins has become an advocate for allowing concealed handgun carry on college campuses.[12] When she experiences pushback from lawmakers bent on "Gun Control," she asks, "How does rendering me defenseless protect you from violent crime?"[13] For most, that question is hard to answer. As an individual American in 2016, cherish your liberty and safety. Don't depend on government to be your first responder. Despite their best intentions, police too often bring body bags and toe tags. Be your *own* first responder and remember that we the American voters are the largest grassroots organization in America. We can join together and show that guns don't have trigger fingers—and that evil is the real problem.

- 11 -

Give A Damn...
Because The IRS Should Host A Bonfire

Taxes are sane or insane. At the beginning of my second year of law school, I was in for lots of reading. For the first half of the year, one of my classes was "Individual Income Tax." Now I had already expected that year to be painful. But when I ordered my books for the tax class, my pain expectations were well exceeded. Like you, I knew our country's tax code was big. "It would fill this many rooms. It's this many words. It's a job killer," we've heard.

One of my books for the class, "Selected Federal Taxation: Statutes and Regulations," weighed in at 1,952 pages.[1] Of course, the keyword was "Selected." The near 2,000 pages of laws and regulations was a mere sampling of our tax code. Bring on the pain train. On the plus side, the book may have been able to stop a bullet. I remember thinking to myself, "No wonder tax lawyers make so much money!" What's the point? It was insane then and it's insane now.

So where did the Internal Revenue Service (IRS) come from? In its original form, the Constitution didn't allow for Congress to impose an individual income tax. But in 1913, Wyoming cast the deciding vote for the 16th Amendment—allowing the federal government to collect an income tax.[2] The first tax code was only 400 pages.[3] At the outset, those making more than $3,000 per year paid only 1 percent. Those making over $500,000 per year paid 7 percent. What a dream world. To pay for World War I in 1918, Congress imposed a top tax rate of 77 percent! The very first individual income tax return was only two pages—four if you included the instructions.[4] The 2014 tax return form and its instructions is 106 pages![5] Sane or insane?

Here in the United States, our system is a progressive income tax. As you may know, individuals who earn more pay higher taxes. Those funds are used to pay for social programs like food stamps and welfare. In conservative-speak, it's effectively "income redistribution." But if the United States didn't have a federal income tax until 1913, what did wealth look like before?

Of course, monopolies ran wild. Guys like Andrew Carnegie, John D. Rockefeller, and Cornelius Vanderbilt did quite well. Rockefeller founded the petroleum monopoly Standard Oil. Unrestrained by a federal income tax, his net worth (in 2014 dollars) was about $340 billion. As a comparison, Bill Gates's net worth is currently $79 billion—a mere fourth of Rockefeller's.[6] America's largest home—the Biltmore Estate in Asheville, North Carolina—was built before the federal income tax.[7]

But here at present day, the tax code and its regulations weigh in at about 75,000 pages. Laid end-to-end, the pages would stretch nearly 13 miles.[8] This begs the question, "Why so long?" The only logical answer is "pure insanity." Our tax system is the best example of our federal government turning a simple issue into complicated beyond comprehension. As you may know, the tax code is full of loopholes for different companies and families.

Generally, singles pay more than married individuals.[9] Is that fair? On the business side, things get more complicated. But first, let's ask ourselves what business owners desire. Generally, they want two things. First, they want certainty in their economy. They want to be able to make wise decisions in a stable business environment. Second, they want their tax burden to be easy to navigate.

In the current environment—especially after Obamacare passed in 2009—neither is the case. The economy is slow and hard to predict. Plus, the tax and regulatory burden has made it hard to start and expand businesses. Imagine for example wanting to expand your business beyond 50 employees, but knowing you'll have to provide all full-time workers with health benefits.[10] For some, that cost to expand is insurmountable.

At the corporate level, America's tax system presents an even more serious problem. The problem makes us less competitive on the world stage. Today, the United States has the highest corporate tax rate in the developed world. No, you didn't go cross-eyed just now. Pretend for a moment that you're the CEO of a large US-based, international company.

Your company has the flexibility to choose anywhere in the world as a headquarters. You're not limited to the U.S. Now, you know that America has the third highest corporate tax rate in the developed world at around 39 percent (at the time of this writing). Countries like Ireland boast 12.5 percent.[11] Outside of a moral desire to remain loyal to the United States, what would you do? Would you move? The logical answer is of course, "Yes." And if you didn't, I'm sure your company's stockholders would make it happen anyway.

> **"Our leadership in Washington has made taxes a nightmare for individuals and a barrier to economic growth for businesses."**

What's the bottom line? Our leadership in Washington has made taxes a nightmare for individuals and a barrier to economic growth for businesses. They've chosen to keep America on the sidelines of growth and global competition. I guess there is one positive here. Tax and accounting firms are happy. That aside, no sane person would call our current situation reasonable. Ask any man or woman working for the IRS why our tax system is so complicated. I guarantee you that none of them could explain it with a clear conscious.

We can do better. What America really needs—and what no leader is willing to do—is a complete, start-to-finish overhaul of the current system. It's time to dump it like a boyfriend or girlfriend in the halls of high school and start over. The way I see it, the U.S. tax system should be simple. It should seek to raise money fairly, efficiently, and wisely. The old system should find itself on a National Mall bonfire. It's time to incinerate the insanity.

Generally, I fall into the "Fair Tax" camp. The idea does away with the entire current system and replaces it with one national, consumption-based tax on retail sales. The more you consume the more you pay and vice versa. Your level of "consumption" is entirely up to you.[12] A Fair Tax system would replace insanity with sanity. It's simple, fair, efficient, and wise. Further, it would shrink the need for the IRS, ensure every American has skin in the game, and ultimately change how we think about taxes. And for those who would miss the old system, realize that the "richest one percent" would still pay more—as they tend to spend more than those who are less fortunate.[13]

More than simplicity, a system like this would empower every American to individually understand their tax burden. The only thing preventing that kind of empowerment is a lack of leadership and the presence of "special interests." Remember, tax and accounting firms thrive because of our tax system's complexity—and they love to pay lobbyists to protect their interests. So when I say that our leaders will need tremendous political might to change that, I'm not joking.

Most politicians running for office talk about "reforming the tax code." Point blank, none of them are serious. None of them harbor the leadership skills or political will to actually pull the trigger. What they mean by "reform" is piecemeal reform—the capital gain tax, tax credits for the middle class, etc. True reform would start from scratch and overcome the special interests. After all, that's what this book is all about: overcoming. This is about what individual Americans can do to change our nation at the national level. It starts with us.

> **"It begins with the realization that our tax burdens are too high, the process is too complicated, and that the power is in the wrong hands."**

I don't care what the tax and accounting lobby has to say. We the American voter are the largest grassroots organization in America. Political labels aside, it begins with conversations in our local communities. It requires boldness. It begins with the realization that our tax burdens are too high, the process is too complicated, and the power is in the wrong hands. This is the one thing that Americans can be ticked off about together. My question is "Why aren't we? Why aren't we mad enough?" We know the system is complicated. We know it isn't fair. We know it's expensive, but we don't act to change it. It's time to give a damn and get vocal. This isn't about right or left and drawing lines in the political sand. It's time to come together for civil and honest conversations about our tax system. Our homes, businesses, and economy are at stake—as well as our global competitiveness. It is time for sanity.

- 12 -

Give A Damn...
Because We'll Unite Despite Our Differences

We're mourning in America. We're divided when we could be united. We're mourning because of racial division and sharp religious disagreements. Look no further than Ferguson, Missouri and Baltimore, Maryland to see toxic race riots and looting. Look no further than Indiana to see Americans on the religious right and liberal left tearing each other apart. To channel Abraham Lincoln, we are a "house divided."[1] To channel Dr. Martin Luther King Jr., we've "succumb to the temptation of bitterness" and allowed our fellow man to "pull [us] so low as to hate him."[2]

As a nation, we're the most divided we've been since the tension and race riots of the 1960s.[3] It's all brokenness. It's all division and will do nothing to restore and unify the American people. We've lost sense of the larger purpose and buried ourselves in short-sighted victories and single-issue debates. It's not politics that have become nasty. Politics have always been nasty. What's become nasty is our inability to lead. What's become nasty is our inability to come together despite our differences.

What's missing from the American conversation is respect, civility, honesty, and ultimately, love for our fellow American. As a nation, our politics have become shallow, superficial, and sensitive. We are separated, divided, and enamored with controversy. What must change is our frame of reference. What must change is the way we view our friends and our enemies. Whether taking to the floor of Congress or stepping in to the local coffee shop, our habits towards one another must change. We can unite despite our differences.

Let's take a look at our country. Let's return to Ferguson, Missouri. In August of 2014, Michael Brown—an unarmed black teenager—was killed in a confrontation with Officer Darren Wilson.[4] Some witnesses said Brown had his hands up in surrender when he was shot. Others said he didn't. The Ferguson police department said that Brown reached for Officer Wilson's gun.[5] Witnesses aside, Brown's death set the streets of Ferguson on fire and brought race issues to forefront of America's mind.

Protests would have been a *desirable* outcome, but what happened was destruction. Instead of seeking honest justice, the news media and those on social media got in their respective corners. Speculation over what happened was rampant. Looting was out of control. Businesses were destroyed and police cars were set on fire. Officer Wilson had to remain in hiding because of death threats. At one point, Missouri Governor Jay Nixon, had to dispatch the National Guard to keep the peace and enforce a mandatory curfew.

In a moment, a small Midwestern town in Missouri became a flashpoint of sharp racial tension. It took weeks for the nightmare to subside. And when a Grand Jury decided not to indict Officer Wilson three months later in November, the riots returned with a vengeance. In March of 2015, two Ferguson police officers were shot as yet another "protest" was dispersing.[6] To this day, I'm not sure the town or America has fully healed. As a nation, we've failed to discuss the real issues with respect, civility, and honesty.

How do I know? Let's take a look at Baltimore, Maryland. On April 12, 2015, police attempted to stop 25-year-old Freddie Gray and another man after they ran from police at an intersection in Baltimore. The police officers caught-up with Gray and arrested him. Witnesses said the officers injured Gray before placing him in a police van. The Police said Gray stopped voluntarily and no force was used. According to the department, one officer took out his Taser, but never used it. But at some point, Freddie Gray's spinal cord was nearly severed and his voice box was crushed.[7] The Baltimore Police Department said that Gray's injuries may have been self-inflicted. However, some doctors disagreed and said that would have required a "significant amount of force"—force akin to that of a car accident.

Ultimately, Gray died April 19, 2015.[8] His arrest and death ignited Ferguson-like riots and looting. The riots continued for days and eventually turned violent. Once again, businesses were destroyed and cars burned. Once again, witnesses, the news media, and those on social media took sides. They went to their corners. Justice wasn't the goal. Respect for the process wasn't the goal. Politically motivated agendas were the goal. Division was the goal. A fractured nation along racial lines was the goal. Unity was not. Unity and healing was lost.

Remember the debate over an Indiana religious freedom bill in February of 2015? It was a bill meant to protect religious freedoms and it was signed into law by Indiana Governor Mike Pence (R).[9] Though the bill was meant to protect religious freedoms, critics called it a license to "discriminate against homosexuals and others."[10] After the bill became law, the owner of Memories Pizza in Walkerton, Indiana, Kevin O'Connor, told a local reporter that he would refuse to cater a gay wedding under the new law.

Following his comments, he was flooded by threatening phone calls and social media attacks. He later clarified his statements by saying he would never refuse service to gay people in his restaurant. But because of his religious convictions, he could not service a gay wedding. Despite trying to clarify his remarks, O'Connor was forced to close his business until the dust settled.[11] A "GoFundMe" campaign later raised $842,000 to support the re-opening of O'Connor's restaurant.[12] During the debate, each side ran to their corners and started slinging mud. There was virtually no respect, civility, or love for one another. There was one beacon of hope, however. One gay woman, Courtney Hoffman, took a bold stand and donated to the GoFundMe campaign. Why? With her donation, Hoffman posted this:

"As a member of the gay community, I would like to apologize for the mean spirited attacks on you and your business. I know many gay individuals who fully support your right to stand up for your beliefs and run your business according to those beliefs. We are outraged at the level of hate and intolerance that has been directed at you and I sincerely hope that you are able to rebuild." [13]

Despite her fundamental disagreement with O'Connor over the definition of marriage, it seems Hoffman understands rights, respect, civility, and love for her fellow American. How refreshing.

So the question becomes, what next? How will America unite despite her differences? What does respect, civility, honesty, and love for our fellow Americans actually look like? First, to dispel with a common misconception, showing respect and creating an environment of civility has nothing to do with compromising our individual values. But it has everything to do with respecting others' ability to freely express themselves and fully explain their ideas honestly. Today our country is entirely too sensitive and too politically correct. As a society, we're thin-skinned and find ourselves shaking in anger when we hear a slight difference of opinion. The natural reaction is for each to run to their respective corners. We have to change that and mentally toughen up. We need to return to the concept that America truly represents an environment where the battle of ideas can be robust and unrestrained.

> **"We need to return to the concept that America truly represents an environment where the battle of ideas can be robust and unrestrained."**

Respect means to show regard or consideration for someone.[14] To me, it means to treat men and women as they were created. Equal. Civility is about creating an environment of courtesy or politeness.[15] To me, it means giving those I disagree with a fair shot in explaining their point of view. Finally, honesty is about showing people who we really are—not shrouding ourselves in the secrecy of sensitivity and political correctness.

Let us come to terms with the fact that we're going to disagree. There are single issues in which some of us will never find resolve. The issue is not that we disagree. The issue is *how* we disagree and *how* we treat each other. It's about the environment we create. It's about the environment we can change. Disagreement and robust debate in America is a good thing. Put simply, we must change how we approach the debate and how we approach our friends *and* foes.

This is about a conscious decision to separate ourselves from the status quo. Not only that, it's about a conscious decision to inspire those around us to separate from the status quo. The status quo is brokenness and divide. It's stagnant, weak, and devoid of principled progress. Ultimately, the status quo has created a bitter vacuum of leadership. We can turn from division and we can do it together. It starts with love for our fellow American—regardless of disagreement. Love for our fellow American has the power to create an environment of respect, civility, and renewed honesty.

> **"The issue is not that we disagree. The issue is *how* we disagree and *how* we treat each other. It's about the environment we create. It's about the environment we can change."**

Our current division and bitterness seems to be ever-present. It stands to destroy our relationships and our nation in the next century. To mark a shift in direction would mean showing compassion for the "other side." It would mean forging friendships with those we would normally sling mud towards. It would mean setting the example for our leaders in Washington. Remember, America's brokenness is her greatest strength. Let us channel it towards restoration.

- 13 -

Give A Damn...
Because Faith Minded Freedom Will Restore

It has become cliché to say that America is broken. It's so cliché that we barely talk about it anymore. For example, our nation's debt hardly ever gets a serious mention in Congress or on television. Instead of addressing it, our leaders choose brokenness. They talk about the threat of ISIS and radical Islamic terror. They stammer at the atrocities committed by the hands of evil, but fail to draft an effective vision and plan to address it.

God forbid America actually *wins* the battle. Instead, our leaders "manage it" and choose brokenness. It would seem our country's priorities are broken too. The administration in Washington consistently and laughably says the greatest threat to America's future is "climate change" – a term lacking in meaning. As a nation, yes, we are broken. So if brokenness is cliché, why do I suggest it is America's greatest strength? Why should we channel brokenness towards restoration?

We know our country's problems. And truthfully, the solution isn't as obvious as fixing the problems. The right solution is more profound, impactful, and longer lasting than quick "fixes." The right solution is to create strength from

America's brokenness—to build faith from a clean slate of ashes. Remember, brokenness is not exclusive to America as a whole. Each of us individually has or is currently experiencing some form of brokenness. Perhaps it was a life or death experience. Maybe it was the loss of a relationship, childhood abuse, or a struggle with addiction. I don't know your brokenness. I only know mine. I know that brokenness increased my faith to take bold steps—and it became my catalyst for growth.

As a nation and as individuals, we've been reduced to ashes. We desire a do-over. We need a clean slate. It's okay to feel that way. That feeling of helplessness and that need for a clean slate has prepared us for refinement. Whatever America has experienced has prepared her for greatness. For you, brokenness has prepared *you* for greatness. Brokenness is power, not weakness. It's a source of motivation and the beginning of renewal and restoration.

Brokenness was the starting point of America's greatest achievements. Our nation's independence began with the angering effects of tyranny. The unity that followed America's Civil War began with bitter division and the near break-up of the United States. The fall of Communism and Ronald Reagan's vision for liberty began with the brokenness of Communism. America found restoration after the heartbreak of 9/11—though it's been a long road.

On the individual level, brokenness has produced amazing achievements. Thomas Edison's light bulb resulted from thousands of failed attempts. Like him or hate him, Glenn Beck's media empire grew from the brokenness of alcoholism and drug addiction.[1] The motivation behind Tony Robbins' career stemmed from childhood poverty and hunger.[2] Though on a smaller scale, my achievements came after losing everything, including a marriage. The summer of 2013 marked the greatest period of brokenness in my life. However, it was the beginning of catalytic growth and what my Creator had planned to launch all along. It was exponential growth. Since then, I've seen more transformation in my life than I ever thought possible. Essentially, God showed me how to channel my brokenness and surround myself with the right people for the future. But before I could channel it correctly, I had to own my brokenness. I had to face it squarely at the root level before I could experience restoration.

If America's restoration were a new skyscraper, brokenness would be the massive hole in the ground before the pouring of the foundation. Brokenness refines us, cleans out the worst from us, and brings out the best in us. It builds our faith from within. It produces vision for the future. For America, we need to reset our focus on robust vision. This is not about being a "City Upon a Hill." It's about more than that and pushing further than that. It's about striving to lead and innovate beyond that.

This is about inspiring leadership in the White House that exceeds our leadership of the past—including George Washington. Why not seek to push the envelope? What's wrong with that? Not a damn thing. Let us be bold and edgy. Let us rid ourselves of the status quo and work together to achieve greatness. This kind of thinking isn't common in American politics, but realize that brokenness must precede restoration. Trials must precede triumphs. Emptiness must precede faith. We've already experienced the brokenness. If we face our nation's brokenness, restoration is within reach—no matter the size of our national debt or the evil around the globe.

> "Brokenness is debilitating, but if the strength and faith we take from brokenness plays the starring role in the story of our country's restoration, we can run from the ashes—even if we first have to crawl."

We have a clean slate of ashes. America is ready to rise to a new vision and better leadership. It's time to sow the seeds of production and prepare the harvest of innovation. Restoration can be ours, but do we desire it enough to square with the root causes of America's brokenness? Are we ready to face our debt, corruption, division, and evil abroad? We have to dig deeper than the surface of our problems. If we want restoration, then it's time to give a damn. If we can give a damn as individuals, then we can set the example for Washington, D.C. As Americans, we can set the true standard for seismic change in the vision that America demonstrates to the world.

As a Christian, one of my favorite pieces of scripture is where Jesus tells us to first love God with all of our heart and second, love others. Despite our disagreements on many issues, we can tap into the power of brokenness, faith, and love for one another. We can bring restoration together and lay aside labels. Brokenness is debilitating, but if the strength and faith we take from brokenness plays the starring role in the story of our country's restoration, we can run from the ashes—even if we first have to crawl. So what does that look like? Where do we go from here? We spend time channeling our brokenness towards restoration, crafting a new vision, and inspiring change from the ground up.

America's best days are yet to come and I'm determined to help lead us towards those days. We don't have to accept the status quo. We can demand different in 2016. Shrugging our shoulders isn't the only response to our country's problems. We can band together through the power of brokenness, faith, and vision. We're not too far gone. We're simply on the sidelines. It's time to get off the bench and bring your personal brokenness to the field—in a way that drives your community and country forward. Whether we're ready or not, 2016 is coming. We can be the skyscraper of restoration or remain buried in our problems. Let us stand, change, and lead together. It's time to give a damn.

- ACKNOWLEDGEMENTS -

I wish to personally thank the following individuals and entities for their support in cultivating the inspiration, knowledge, and wisdom that went into this book.

To my parents, sister, and extended family for raising one pain in the butt son. You molded me into the man I could have never thought to be on my own. Our Creator used each of you to radically impact my life in times of triumph, tragedy, victory, and setback. I love each of you dearly.

To Gabrielle Bosché for being the Bride that I would have never known to ask for, pray for, or look for. You are truly my greatest helper. Your honesty, support, grace, and love compel me to give you my best everyday. We're only getting started.

To Tyler Lucas for being my brother, friend, confidant, and best advisor. My gratitude is hardly sufficient to thank you for the research in this book and your perspective on the approach. You might think it is I who inspires you. Let me be the first to tell you that it is *you* who inspires me. Cheers to you, my brother. We're too are only getting started.

To New York Times Bestselling Author, Tamara Lowe, for being an instrument of sea change in my life at the most important time. You took a young man who only knew how to speak well on camera and you turned him into businessman.

Besides my Creator, my bride, and my family, you radically changed my perspective on achieving my goals and dreams.

To FOX News Channel White House Correspondent, Kevin Corke, for giving me a leg up in national media. Your mentorship helped to inspire the tenacity and strong will it takes to survive in national politics and media. More than anything, you're one of my closest friends. You're the gold standard in friendship and mentorship.

To Brandon and Jared Vallorani for giving me the opportunity to bring *13 Reasons To Give A Damn In 2016* to your amazing subscribers. I esteem most your friendship, advice, and support. You two gentlemen and your amazing company, Liberty Alliance, has radically changed the pace my life. Thanks for giving me a shot.

To George Tyler Jones of Liberty Alliance for helping me scale up Give A Damn Coffee. Your advice, friendship, and honesty in business is refreshing.

To Liz Darnell of Liberty Alliance for thinking of building the brand Give-A-Damn Coffee. One conversation at CPAC in 2015 made for one incredible concept.

To Tamara Holder for your advice and insight as a FOX News Contributor. Despite your liberal leanings and crazy arguments on Hannity, I love you nonetheless. You make me laugh at least once per week.

To Glenn Beck, Joel Cheatwood, Joe Weasel, Ryan Cost, and TheBlaze for giving me the opportunity to understand investigative journalism on a national level. The principles of vision that you gentlemen instilled in me will last a lifetime.

To Robert Earls for being that friend who picked me up off the floor when I was at my worst. The friend you have been to my family has inspired me to give my very best in every relationship. You're a true gentleman.

To Robert Ross for giving me "no B.S." advice and kicking my butt to victory in every area of life. I owe you cup a of joe at Mill Mountain Coffee, my friend.

To Dr. Robert Vogel for seeing the very best in me as I finished out law school. You encouraged me to go after my dreams to change the very face of politics and media when I was ready to throw in the towel. I seek to make you proud, my friend.

To Danny Guymon and Donald Walker for being the closest of friends. It's so good to be living in District next to you, gentlemen.

To the late Doug Chase for your service to America in Vietnam. You deserved to be honored with more than a scheduling scandal at the VA Hospital System. Sadly, I never got the opportunity to meet you. Your story made an indelible impact on my heart. Rest in peace, kind sir.

To Suzanne Chase, wife of Doug Chase, for being an incredible American. Listening to you tell the story of your husband's life and the story of his final days, broke my heart and moved me change our nation for the better. May God honor your commitment to ending bureaucratic corruption. Keep telling your husband's story, Suzanne. I've got your back.

To the visionary founder of Turning Point USA, Charlie Kirk, for your perspective on Chapter 8, "Give A Damn... Because Student Debt Stalls the American Dream." Your level of motivation and commitment to changing America from the ground up truly inspires me. You very obviously "give a damn."

To Crayle Vanest, Assistant Director of Development at Students for Concealed Carry, for your perspective in Chapter 10, "Give A Damn... Because Guns Don't Have Trigger Fingers" and for your work to educate young Americans about firearms, owning their personal safety, and being their own first responders.

NOTES

- CHAPTER ONE -

[1] "State-by-State Ratification Table | Teaching American History." Teaching American History. Ashbrook Center, 20 Dec. 2014. Web. 17 June 2015. <http://teachingamericanhistory.org/ratification/overview/.

[2] U.S. Constitution. Art. V.

[3] "The Constitution of the United States: America's Founding Fathers." National Archives and Records Administration. National Archives and Records Administration, n.d. Web. 20 Dec. 2014. <http://www.archives.gov/exhibits/charters/constitution_founding_fat hers_new_hampshire.html>.

[4] "State-by-State Ratification Table | Teaching American History." Teaching American History. Ashbrook Center, 20 Dec. 2014. Web. 17 June 2015. <http://teachingamericanhistory.org/ratification/overview/.

[5] Weisman, Jonathan, and Ashley Parker. "Riding Wave of Discontent, G.O.P. Takes Senate." The New York Times. The New York Times, 04 Nov. 2014. Web. 20 June 2014. <http://www.nytimes.com/2014/11/05/us/politics/midterm-elections.html?_r=0>.

[6] "Exclusive: Sen. Mitch McConnell Lays out New Senate's Agenda." Fox News. FOX News Network, 09 Jan. 2015. Web. 20 Dec. 2014. <http://www.foxnews.com/transcript/2015/01/09/exclusive-sen-mitch-mcconnell-lays-out-new-senate-agenda/>.

[7] "Presidential Candidates Debates: Presidential Debate in New York." Presidential Candidates Debates: Presidential Debate in New York. The American Presidency Project, n.d. Web. 20 Dec. 2014. <http://www.presidency.ucsb.edu/ws/?pid=29403>.

[8] "Abraham Lincoln: Second Inaugural Address. U.S. Inaugural Addresses. 1989." Abraham Lincoln: Second Inaugural Address. U.S. Inaugural Addresses. 1989. N.p., n.d. Web. 20 Dec. 2014. <http://www.bartleby.com/124/pres32.html>.

– CHAPTER TWO –

[1] "Definition of Incompetence in English:." Incompetence: Definition of Incompetence in Oxford Dictionary (American English) (US). Oxford Dictionary Press, n.d. Web. 20 Dec. 2014. <http://www.oxforddictionaries.com/us/definition/american_english/incompetence>.

[2] "Definition of Corruption in English:." Corruption: Definition of Corruption in Oxford Dictionary (American English) (US). Oxford Dictionary Press, n.d. Web. 20 Dec. 2014. <http://www.oxforddictionaries.com/us/definition/american_english/corruption>.

[3] "VA Bonuses Were Incentive to Hide Wait Times, Whistleblowers Say." CBSNews. CBS Interactive, n.d. Web. 10 Jan. 2015. <http://www.cbsnews.com/news/va-bonuses-tied-to-secret-waiting-lists-whistleblower-says/>.

[4] "A Fatal Wait: Veterans Languish and Die on a VA Hospital's Secret List - CNN.com." CNN. Cable News Network, n.d. Web. 10 Jan. 2015. <http://www.cnn.com/2014/04/23/health/veterans-dying-health-care-delays/>.

[5] Harris, Craig, and Rob O'Dell. "Phoenix VA Gave out $10 Mil in Bonuses in past 3 Years." AZ Central. Gannett Company, 17 June 2014. Web. 10 Dec. 2015.
<http://www.azcentral.com/story/news/arizona/investigations/2014/06/17/phoenix-va-gave-mil-bonuses-last-years/10653263/>.

[6] Bump, Philip. "Why Couldn't Hillary Clinton Have Two E-mail Accounts on One Phone?" Washington Post. The Washington Post, 10 Mar. 2015. Web. 17 June 2015.
<http://www.washingtonpost.com/blogs/the-fix/wp/2015/03/10/why-couldnt-hillary-clinton-have-two-email-accounts-on-one-phone/>.

[7] Frates, Chris. "More than 1,200 Clinton Emails Deemed 'personal' - CNNPolitics.com." CNN. Cable News Network, 21 May 2015. Web. 1 June 2015. <http://www.cnn.com/2015/05/21/politics/hillary-clinton-1200-emails-state-department/>.

[8] Schouten, Fredreka. "Clinton Wipes Server after Handing over E-mails." USA Today. Gannett, 28 Mar. 2015. Web. 1 May 2015.
<http://www.usatoday.com/story/news/politics/2015/03/28/hillary-clinton-emails/70583404/>.

[9] Brennan, Margaret, and Steve Chaggaris. "Hillary Clinton's Team Defends Her Email Usage during Her Tenure at State." CBSNews. CBS Interactive, 3 Mar. 2015. Web. 1 June 2015.
<http://www.cbsnews.com/news/hillary-clintons-team-defends-her-email-usage-at-state/>.

- CHAPTER THREE -

[1] "House Passes $1.1 Trillion Spending Bill after Week of Drama." POLITICO. Politico LLC, 12 Dec. 2015. Web. 14 Jan. 2015.

<http://www.politico.com/story/2014/12/2015-gop-budget-back-up-plan-113498.html>.

[2] "Federal Debt Limit Comes Back into Force at $18.1 Trillion." FOX News. FOX News Network, LLC, 17 Mar. 2015. Web. 1 Apr. 2015. <http%3A%2F%2Fwww.foxnews.com%2Fpolitics%2F2015%2F03%2F17%2Ffederal-debt-limit-comes-back-into-force-at-181-trillion%2F>.

[3] Chappell, Bill. "'Cromnibus' Spending Bill Passes, Just Hours Before Deadline." NPR. NPR, 11 Dec. 2014. Web. 10 Jan. 2015. <http://www.npr.org/sections/thetwo-way/2014/12/11/370132039/house-poised-to-vote-on-controversial-cromnibus-spending-bill>.

[4] Garver, Rob. "5 More Surprises Hiding in the CRomnibus Bill." The Fiscal Times. The Fiscal Times, 26 Dec. 2014. Web. 10 Jan. 2015. <http://www.thefiscaltimes.com/2014/12/26/5-More-Surprises-Hiding-CRomnibus-Bill>.

[5] Morgan, John. "Reagan Adviser David Stockman: Towering Federal Debt Is Hidden in a 'Roach Motel'" Newsmax. Newsmax Media, Inc., 08 Dec. 2014. Web. 10 Jan. 2015. <http://www.newsmax.com/Finance/Stockman-debt-GDP-federal/2014/12/08/id/611723/>.

[6] Chappell, Bill. "'Cromnibus' Spending Bill Passes, Just Hours Before Deadline." NPR. NPR, 11 Dec. 2014. Web. 10 Jan. 2015. <http://www.npr.org/sections/thetwo-way/2014/12/11/370132039/house-poised-to-vote-on-controversial-cromnibus-spending-bill>.

[7] U.S. Constitution. Amend. I.

[8] "Definition of Wisdom in English:." Wisdom: Definition of Wisdom in Oxford Dictionary (American English) (US). Oxfor University

Press, n.d. Web. 10 Jan. 2015.
<http://www.oxforddictionaries.com/us/definition/american_english/wisdom>.

[9] Jefferson, Thomas. "Thomas Jefferson to Richard Price." Letter to Richard Price. 08 Jan. 1789. Library of Congress. N.p., n.d. Web. 10 Jan. 2015. <http://www.loc.gov/exhibits/jefferson/60.html>.

- CHAPTER FOUR -

[1] Weiner, Rachel. "'The Life of Julia' and the New Frontiers of Presidential Politics." Washington Post. The Washington Post, 03 May 2012. Web. 18 Jan. 2015. <http://www.washingtonpost.com/blogs/the-fix/post/the-life-of-julia-shows-obama-camps-web-savvy/2012/05/03/gIQAIy1YzT_blog.html>.

[2] Gregory, Paul. "President Obama's Legacy: $20 Trillion in Debt for 2016 Victor." Forbes. Forbes Magazine, 25 Dec. 2012. Web. 17 June 2015. <http://www.forbes.com/sites/paulroderickgregory/2012/12/25/president-obamas-legacy-20-trillion-in-deficits-for-2016-victor/>.

[3] Boccia, Romina. "Federal Spending by the Numbers, 2014: Government Spending Trends in Graphics, Tables, and Key Points (Including 51 Examples of Government Waste)." The Heritage Foundation. N.p., 8 Dec. 2014. Web. 18 Jan. 2015. <http://www.heritage.org/research/reports/2014/12/federal-spending-by-the-numbers-2014>.

[4] "Databases, Tables & Calculators by Subject." Bureau of Labor Statistics Data. U.S. Bureau of Labor Statistics, 17 June 2015. Web. 17 June 2015. <http://data.bls.gov/timeseries/LNS14000000>.

[5] Jacobson, Louis. "Barack Obama Says Unemployment Rate Now Lower than before the Financial Crisis of 2008." Politifact. Tampa Bay Times, 21 Jan. 2015. Web. 25 Jan. 2015. <http://www.politifact.com/truth-o-meter/statements/2015/jan/21/barack-obama/barack-obama-says-unemployment-rate-now-lower-fina/>.

[6] Berkowitz, Ben. "Chart: What's the Real Unemployment Rate?" CNBC. CNBC LLC, 03 Apr. 2015. Web. 1 May 2015. <http://www.cnbc.com/id/102559454>.

[7] "Quantitative Easing Definition | Investopedia." Investopedia. Investopedia LLC, 12 Apr. 2009. Web. 18 Jan. 2015. <http://www.investopedia.com/terms/q/quantitative-easing.asp>.

[8] "Fed Bond Buying Is Weakening the Dollar: Study." CNBC. CNBC LLC, 01 Apr. 2013. Web. 18 Jan. 2015. <http://www.cnbc.com/id/100606680>.

[9] "Liquidity Definition | Investopedia." Investopedia. Investopedia LLC, 23 Nov. 2003. Web. 18 Jan. 2015. <http://www.investopedia.com/terms/l/liquidity.asp>.

[10] "Quantitative Easing Definition | Investopedia." Investopedia. Investopedia LLC, 12 Apr. 2009. Web. 18 June 2015. <http://www.investopedia.com/terms/q/quantitative-easing.asp>.

[11] "Timeline: A Short History of QE and the Market - Marketwatch." MarketWatch. MarketWatch, Inc., 25 Nov. 2008. Web. 18 Jan. 2015. <http://projects.marketwatch.com/short-history-of-qe-and-the-market-timeline/#>.

[12] Monaghan, Angela. "US Federal Reserve to End Quantitative Easing Programme." The Guardian. Guardian News and Media Limited, 29 Oct. 2014. Web. 18 Jan. 2015. <http%3A%2F%2Fwww.theguardian.com%2Fbusiness%2F2014%2F

oct%2F29%2Fus-federal-reserve-end-quantitative-easing-programme>.

[13] Snyder, Michael. "The 9 Reasons Why Quantitative Easing Is Bad For The U.S. Economy." Business Insider. Business Insider, Inc, 05 Nov. 2010. Web. 18 Jan. 2015. <http://www.businessinsider.com/why-quantitative-easing-is-bad-for-the-economy-2010-11>.

[14] Obama, Barack. "State of the Union Address." State of The Union. U.S. Capitol, Washington, D.C. 20 Jan. 2015. Address.

[15] Mathur, Aparna, and Abby McCloskey. "Fostering Upward Economic Mobility in the United States." AEI. American Enterprise Institute for Public Policy Research, 19 Mar. 2014. Web. 18 Jan. 2015. <https://www.aei.org/publication/fostering-upward-economic-mobility-in-the-united-states/>.

[16] Pomerleau, Kyle, and Andrew Lundeen. "The U.S. Has the Highest Corporate Income Tax Rate in the OECD." Tax Foundation. N.p., 27 Jan. 2014. Web. 18 June 2015. <http://taxfoundation.org/blog/us-has-highest-corporate-income-tax-rate-oecd>.

[17] "Country Rankings." 2015 Index of Economic Freedom. The Heritage Foundation in Partnership with Wall Street Journal, n.d. Web. 18 Jan. 2015. <http://www.heritage.org/index/ranking>.

[18] "Executive Summary." Index of Economic Freedom (2008): n. pag. 2015 Index of Economic Freedom. The Heritage Foundation in Partnership with Wall Street Journal, 2008. Web. 18 Jan. 2015. <http://thf_media.s3.amazonaws.com/index/pdf/2008/Index2008_ExecutiveSummary.pdf>.

[19] "United States Economy: Population, GDP, Unemployment, Inflation, Spending." 2015 Index of Economic Freedom. The Heritage

---

Foundation in Partnership with Wall Street Journal, n.d. Web. 18 Jan. 2015. <http://www.heritage.org/index/country/unitedstates>.

[20] "Milton Friedman in His Own Words." Becker Friedman Institute. The University of Chicago, 9 Nov. 2012. Web. 18 Jan. 2015. <https://bfi.uchicago.edu/post/milton-friedman-his-own-words>.

[21] "Milton Friedman in His Own Words." Becker Friedman Institute. The University of Chicago, 9 Nov. 2012. Web. 18 Jan. 2015. <https://bfi.uchicago.edu/post/milton-friedman-his-own-words>.

– CHAPTER FIVE –

[1] Levs, Josh, Ed Payne, and Michael Pearson. "A Timeline of the Charlie Hebdo Terror Attack - CNN.com." CNN. Cable News Network, 9 Jan. 2015. Web. 21 Jan. 2015. <http://www.cnn.com/2015/01/08/europe/charlie-hebdo-attack-timeline/>.

[2] Goldstein, Sasha. "Charlie Hebdo's Long History of Provocative Religious Satire." NY Daily News. N.p., 7 Jan. 2015. Web. 21 June 2015. <http://www.nydailynews.com/news/crime/charlie-hebdo-long-history-provocative-religious-satire-article-1.2068634>.

[3] "What Is Charlie Hebdo and Why Was the Magazine Targeted? – The Short Answer." The Wall Street Journal. Dow Jones & Company, 7 Jan. 2015. Web. 21 Jan. 2015. <http://blogs.wsj.com/briefly/2015/01/07/what-is-charlie-hebdo-and-why-was-the-magazine-targeted-the-short-answer/>.

[4] Vinograd, Cassandra, Alastair Jamieson, Florence Viala, and Alexander Smith. "Charlie Hebdo Shooting: 12 Killed at Muhammad Cartoons Magazine in Paris." NBC News. N.p., 7 Jan. 2015. Web. 17 June 2015. <http://www.nbcnews.com/storyline/paris-magazine-

attack/charlie-hebdo-shooting-12-killed-muhammad-cartoons-magazine-paris-n281266>.

[5] "Workers Hide on Rooftop from Machine Gunfire in Paris Charlie Hebdo Attack." The Telegraph. Telegraph Media Group, 7 Jan. 2015. Web. 21 Jan. 2015.
<http://www.telegraph.co.uk/news/worldnews/europe/france/1133028 8/Workers-hide-on-rooftop-from-machine-gunfire-in-Paris-Charlie-Hebdo-attack.html>.

[6] Thompson, Catherine. "GRAPHIC VIDEO: Gunmen Shoot Police Officer During Charlie Hebdo Attack." Talking Points Memo. TPM Media LLC, 7 Jan. 2015. Web. 21 Jan. 2015.
<http://talkingpointsmemo.com/livewire/charlie-hebdo-gunmen-video-police-officer-shot>.

[7] Fredericks, Bob. "Charlie Hebdo Terrorists Separated Men and Women before Executions." New York Post. NYP Holdings, Inc, 9 Jan. 2015. Web. 17 June 2015.
<http://nypost.com/2015/01/09/charlie-hebdo-terrorists-separated-men-and-women-before-executions/>.

[8] Saul, Heather. "Paris Attacks Timeline: From Charlie Hebdo to a Jewish Grocery Store - How Two Hostage Situations Unfolded." The Independent. N.p., 9 Jan. 2015. Web. 21 June 2015.
<http://www.independent.co.uk/news/world/europe/paris-attacks-timeline-from-charlie-hebdo-to-dammartinengoele--how-the-double-hostage-situation-unfolded-9968543.html>.

[9] Jolly, David. "Satirical Magazine Is Firebombed in Paris." The New York Times. The New York Times, 02 Nov. 2011. Web. 21 Jan. 2015. <http://www.nytimes.com/2011/11/03/world/europe/charlie-hebdo-magazine-in-paris-is-firebombed.html?_r=0>.

Notes

[10] Ritchie, Meabh. "'I'd Rather Die Standing than Live on My Knees': Charlie Hebdo, Told in Quotes." The Telegraph. Telegraph Media Group, 08 Jan. 2015. Web. 21 June 2015. <http://www.telegraph.co.uk/news/worldnews/europe/france/1133325 0/Id-rather-die-standing-than-live-on-my-knees-Charlie-Hebdo-told-in-quotes.html>.

[11] "Benjamin Netanyahu, Mahmoud Abbas Join Unity Rally." Msnbc.com. NBC News Digital, 11 Jan. 2015. Web. 21 Jan. 2015. <http://www.msnbc.com/up/watch/netanyahu--abbas-join-paris-unity-rally-382918723516>.

[12] "ISNA President: Imam Mohamed Magid." ISNA. Islamic Society of North America, n.d. Web. 21 Jan. 2015. <http://www.isna.net/mohamed-magid.html>.

[13] "Holy Land Foundation Terror-Financing Trial - Documents." ClarionProject.org. Clarion Project, Inc., 20 Oct. 2015. Web. 17 June 2015. <http://www.clarionproject.org/news/holy-land-foundation-terror-financing-trial-documents>.

[14] "ISNA President at White House Iftar." ISNA. Islamic Society of North America, n.d. Web. 21 Jan. 2015. <http://www.isna.net/isna-president-at-white-house-iftar.html>.

[15] Khan, Fahad. "Message from President Obama for ISNA Convention." YouTube. N.p., 31 Aug. 2013. Web. 21 June 2015. <https://www.youtube.com/watch?v=PnS9-pm8vCY>.

[16] "Terrorists Bomb Trains in Madrid." History.com. A&E Television Networks, n.d. Web. 21 Jan. 2015. <http://www.history.com/this-day-in-history/terrorists-bomb-trains-in-madrid>.

[17] "Terrorists Attack London Transit System at Rush Hour." History.com. A&E Television Networks, n.d. Web. 21 Jan. 2015.

<http://www.history.com/this-day-in-history/terrorists-attack-london-transit-system-at-rush-hour>.

[18] O'connor, Anahad, and Eric Schmitt. "Terror Attempt Seen as Man Tries to Ignite Device on Jet." The New York Times. The New York Times, 25 Dec. 2009. Web. 21 Jan. 2015. <http://www.nytimes.com/2009/12/26/us/26plane.html>.

[19] Baker, Al, and William K. Rashbaum. "Police Find Car Bomb in Times Square." The New York Times. The New York Times, 01 May 2010. Web. 21 June 2015. <http://www.nytimes.com/2010/05/02/nyregion/02timessquare.html?pagewanted=all>.

[20] "Army Major Kills 13 People in Fort Hood Shooting Spree." History.com. A&E Television Networks, n.d. Web. 21 Jan. 2015. <http://www.history.com/this-day-in-history/army-major-kills-13-people-in-fort-hood-shooting-spree>.

[21] Daly, Michael. "Nidal Hasan's Murders Termed 'Workplace Violence' by U.S." The Daily Beast. The Daily Beast Company, LLC, 6 Aug. 2013. Web. 21 Jan. 2015. <http://www.thedailybeast.com/articles/2013/08/06/nidal-hasan-s-murders-termed-workplace-violence-by-u-s.html>.

[22] Howden, Daniel. "Terror in Westgate Mall: The Full Story of the Attacks That Devastated Kenya." The Guardian. Guardian News and Media Limited, 4 Oct. 2013. Web. 21 Jan. 2015. <http%3A%2F%2Fwww.theguardian.com%2Fworld%2Finteractive%2F2013%2Foct%2F04%2Fwestgate-mall-attacks-kenya-terror>.

[23] "Sharia Law." The Free Dictionary. Farlex, Inc., n.d. Web. 21 Jan. 2015. <http://www.thefreedictionary.com/sharia+law>.

[24] Spencer, Robert. "American Muslim Writer: Islam Rejects Lying and Deception in All Forms, except When It Doesn't." Jihad Watch.

Free Speech Defense, 11 Jan. 2008. Web. 21 Jan. 2015.
<http://www.jihadwatch.org/2008/01/american-muslim-writer-islam-rejects-lying-and-deception-in-all-forms-except-when-it-doesnt>.

[25] Banco, Erin. "In Coup Attempt, Yemeni Houthi Rebels Take Over Palace, President Hadi's Location Still Unknown." International Business Times. IBT Media Inc., 20 Jan. 2015. Web. 21 Jan. 2015.
<http://www.ibtimes.com/coup-attempt-yemeni-houthi-rebels-take-over-palace-president-hadis-location-still-1788978>.

[26] Carter, Sara. "Arizona Ranchers Say Mexican Drug Lords Rule in U.S. Border Regions: 'We're Living By the Law Of the Cartels'." TheBlaze. N.p., 12 Sept. 2013. Web. 21 Jan. 2015.
<http://www.theblaze.com/stories/2013/09/12/arizona-ranchers-say-mexican-drug-lords-rule-in-u-s-border-regions-were-living-by-the-law-of-the-cartels/>.

[27] Carter, Sara. "The Odd Book One Texas Rancher Found Near the Border." TheBlaze. N.p., 14 July 2014. Web. 21 Jan. 2015.
<http://www.theblaze.com/stories/2014/07/14/urdu-dictionary-found-on-texas-ranch-near-border-we-just-dont-know-whos-here-already/>.

[28] Macke, Tricia, Amy Wagner, Jody Barr, and Lisa Hutson. "Terror Suspect Christopher Cornell: "I'm so Dedicated That I Risked My Whole Life"" Fox 19 Now. WorldNow, 9 Mar. 2015. Web. 21 June 2015. <http://www.fox19.com/story/28284966/cornell-the-planned-attack-against-the-united-states-capitol-the-event-in-which-i-planned-was-but-a-reaction-to-the-continued-american-aggression>.

[29] Sorkin, Aaron. "The Newsroom Script Episode 1 Quotes." GoodReads. N.p., n.d. Web. 21 Jan. 2015.
<http://www.goodreads.com/work/quotes/23633463-the-newsroom-script-episode-1>.

[30] Guandolo, John. "Refusal by Our Leaders to Know the Enemy and Destroy Them Leads to Catastrophic Consequences." The Counter Jihad Report. N.p., 12 June 2014. Web. 21 Jan. 2015. <http://counterjihadreport.com/2014/06/12/refusal-by-our-leaders-to-know-the-enemy-and-destroy-them-leads-to-catastrophic-consequences/>.

- CHAPTER SIX -

[1] Smith, Malcolm. "The Projection of War, 1918 TO 1939." Britain and 1940: History, Myth, and Popular Memory. London: Routledge, 2000. 22-23. Print.

[2] "Pan-Germanism." Encyclopædia Britannica. N.d. Web. 17 June 2015. <http://www.britannica.com/event/Pan-Germanism>.

[3] "Germany Annexes Austria." History.com. A&E Television Networks, n.d. Web. 24 Jan. 2015. <http://www.history.com/this-day-in-history/germany-annexes-austria>.

[4] "Munich Agreement." Encyclopædia Britannica. N.p., 10 Feb. 2015. Web. 17 June 2015. <http://www.britannica.com/event/Munich-Agreement>.

[5] Chen, C. Peter. "Munich Conference and the Annexation of Sudetenland." World War II Database. Lava Development, LLC, n.d. Web. 17 June 2015. <http://ww2db.com/battle_spec.php?battle_id=87>.

[6] Chamberlain, Neville. "Peace For Our Time." 10 Downing Street, London. Brigham Young University. Web. 17 June 2015. <http://eudocs.lib.byu.edu/index.php/Neville_Chamberlain's_%22Peace_For_Our_Time%22_speech>.

[7] "Nazis Take Czechoslovakia." History.com. A&E Television Networks, n.d. Web. 17 June 2015. <http://www.history.com/this-day-in-history/nazis-take-czechoslovakia>.

[8] "Germany Invades Poland." History.com. A&E Television Networks, n.d. Web. 24 Jan. 2015. <http://www.history.com/this-day-in-history/germany-invades-poland>.

[9] "Declaration of War: PM Neville Chamberlain Announces Britain Is at War." BBC. N.p., n.d. Web. 21 Jan. 2015.

<http://www.bbc.co.uk/learning/schoolradio/subjects/history/ww2clips/speeches/chamberlain_declares_war>.

[10] "Churchill Becomes Prime Minister." History.com. A&E Television Networks, n.d. Web. 21 Jan. 2015.

<http://www.history.com/this-day-in-history/churchill-becomes-prime-minister>.

[11] Churchill, Winston. "Blood, Toil, Tears, and Sweat." Palace of Westminster, London. 13 May 1940. The Churchill Centre. Web. 21 Jan. 2015.

<http://www.winstonchurchill.org/resources/speeches/1940-the-finest-hour/blood-toil-tears-and-sweat>.

[12] Carruthers, Wanda. "Bolton: US Sanctions Against Russia 'So Weak It's Embarrassing'" Newsmax. Newsmax Media, Inc., 17 Mar. 2014. Web. 21 Jan. 2015.

<http://www.newsmax.com/Newsfront/Bolton-sanctions-Putin-Russia/2014/03/17/id/560047/>.

[13] Zoroya, Gregg. "Rebels Capture Yemen Presidential Palace, Shell Residence." <i>USA Today</i>. Gannett, 20 Jan. 2015. Web. 21 Jan. 2015.

<http://www.usatoday.com/story/news/world/2015/01/20/yemen-shiite-rebels/22038397/>.

[14] Bergsten, C. Fred. "Currency Manipulation: Why Something Must Be Done." Forbes. Forbes Magazine, 25 Feb. 2015. Web. 1 Mar. 2015. <http://www.forbes.com/sites/realspin/2015/02/25/currency-manipulation-why-something-must-be-done/>.

[15] "USSR Established." History.com. A&E Television Networks, n.d. Web. 21 Jan. 2015. <http://www.history.com/this-day-in-history/ussr-established>.

[16] "Ukrainian Independence." Worldwide News Ukraine. N.p., n.d. Web. 21 Jan. 2015. <http://wnu-ukraine.com/about-ukraine/history/ukrainian-independence/>.

[17] France-Presse, Agence. "Vladimir Putin Describes Secret Meeting When Russia Decided to Seize Crimea." The Guardian. Guardian News and Media Limited, 9 Mar. 2015. Web. 24 Jan. 2015. <http%3A%2F%2Fwww.theguardian.com%2Fworld%2F2015%2Fmar%2F09%2Fvladimir-putin-describes-secret-meeting-when-russia-decided-to-seize-crimea>.

[18] "Russia Leader Vladimir Putin Says He'll Protect Russians in Ukraine by Any Means, but Hopes Force Not Required." CBS News. CBS Interactive Inc., 4 Mar. 2014. Web. 24 Jan. 2015. <http://www.cbsnews.com/news/putin-reportedly-orders-troops-near-ukraine-border-back-to-bases-after-military-exercises/>.

[19] Abdullah, Halimah. "Crimea's Vote: Was It Legal?" CNN. Cable News Network, 19 Mar. 2014. Web. 24 Mar. 2015. <http://www.cnn.com/2014/03/17/world/europe/ukraine-vote-legality/>.

[20] Welsh, Teresea. "Putin Defends Actions in Ukraine." U.S. News & World Report. U.S. News & World Report LP, 4 Dec. 2014. Web. 24 Jan. 2015. <http%3A%2F%2Fwww.usnews.com%2Fnews%2Farticles%2F2014

%2F12%2F04%2Frussian-president-vladimir-putin-asserts-right-to-crimea-in-ukraine>.

[21] "Putin Orders Russian Troop Withdrawal from Ukrainian Border." Reuters. Thomson Reuters, 12 Oct. 2014. Web. 24 Jan. 2015. <http://www.reuters.com/article/2014/10/12/us-ukraine-crisis-putin-military-idUSKCN0I103V20141012>.

[22] Zoroya, Gregg. "Rebels Capture Yemen Presidential Palace, Shell Residence." USA Today. Gannett, 20 Jan. 2015. Web. 24 Jan. 2015. <http://www.usatoday.com/story/news/world/2015/01/20/yemen-shiite-rebels/22038397/>.

[23] Taylor, Adam. "Four Months Ago, Obama Called Yemen's War on Terror a Success. Now the Yemeni Government May Fall." Washington Post. The Washington Post, 20 Jan. 2015. Web. 24 June 2015. <http://www.washingtonpost.com/blogs/worldviews/wp/2015/01/20/four-months-ago-obama-called-yemens-war-on-terror-a-success-now-the-yemeni-government-may-fall/>.

[24] Engel, Pamela. "Obama Just Made His Clearest Statement Yet on Iran's Support of Terrorism." Business Insider. Business Insider, Inc, 13 May 2015. Web. 1 June 2015. <http://www.businessinsider.com/obama-iran-is-a-state-sponsor-of-terrorism-2015-5>.

[25] Tacopino, Joe. "Iran's Supreme Leader Screams 'Death to America' amid Ongoing Nuclear Talks." New York Post. NYP Holdings, Inc, 23 Mar. 2015. Web. 1 Apr. 2015. <http://nypost.com/2015/03/23/irans-supreme-leader-screams-death-to-america-amid-ongoing-nuclear-talks/>.

[26] "Statement by the President on the Framework to Prevent Iran from Obtaining a Nuclear Weapon." The White House. The White House,

2 Apr. 2015. Web. 1 June 2015. <https://www.whitehouse.gov/the-press-office/2015/04/02/statement-president-framework-prevent-iran-obtaining-nuclear-weapon>.

[27] Walsh, Deirdre. "Iran: No Signing Final Nuclear Deal Unless Economic Sanctions Are Lifted." CNN. Cable News Network, 9 Apr. 2015. Web. 1 June 2015. <http://www.cnn.com/2015/04/09/politics/iran-nuclear-bill/>.

- CHAPTER SEVEN -

[1] Smith, Emily, and Caitlin Stark. "By the Numbers: Health Insurance - CNNPolitics.com." CNN. Cable News Network, 28 June 2012. Web. 30 Jan. 2015. <http://www.cnn.com/2012/06/27/politics/btn-health-care/>.

[2] Stolberg, Sheryl Gay, and Robert Pear. "Obama Signs Health Care Overhaul Bill, With a Flourish." The New York Times. The New York Times, 23 Mar. 2010. Web. 30 Jan. 2015. <http://www.nytimes.com/2010/03/24/health/policy/24health.html>.

[3] "Health Insurance Coverage For Children and Young Adults Under 26." HealthCare.gov. Medicare & Medicaid Services, n.d. Web. 30 Jan. 2015. <https://www.healthcare.gov/young-adults/children-under-26/>.

[4] "Rights and Protections." HealthCare.gov. Medicare & Medicaid Services, n.d. Web. 30 Jan. 2015. <https://www.healthcare.gov/health-care-law-protections/>.

[5] "ObamaCare Individual Mandate." Obamacare Facts. N.p., n.d. Web. 30 Jan. 2015. <http://obamacarefacts.com/obamacare-individual-mandate/>.

[6] "ObamaCare Employer Mandate." Obamacare Facts. N.p., n.d. Web. 30 Jan. 2015. <http://obamacarefacts.com/obamacare-employer-mandate/>.

[7] Murphy, Shailagh, and Lori Montgomery. "House Passes Health-care Reform Bill without Republican Votes." Washington Post. The Washington Post, 22 Mar. 2010. Web. 30 Jan. 2015. <http://www.washingtonpost.com/wp-dyn/content/article/2010/03/21/AR2010032100943.html>.

[8] Radnofsky, Louise. "Poorly Managed HealthCare.gov Construction Cost $840 Million, Watchdog Finds." The Wall Street Journal. Dow Jones & Company, 30 July 2014. Web. 30 Jan. 2015. <http://www.wsj.com/articles/poorly-managed-healthcare-gov-construction-cost-840-million-watchdog-finds-1406751529>.

[9] "ObamaCare Deficit and Debt." Obamacare Facts. N.p., n.d. Web. 30 Jan. 2015. <http://obamacarefacts.com/obamacare-deficit-debt/>.

[10] Gottlieb, Scott. "How Much Does Obamacare Rip Off Young Adults? We Ran The Numbers. Here Are The Results." Forbes. N.p., 28 Mar. 2014. Web. 30 Jan. 2015. <http://www.forbes.com/sites/scottgottlieb/2014/03/28/how-much-does-obamacare-rip-off-generation-x-we-ran-the-numbers-here-are-the-results/>.

[11] Sherfinski, David. "Ezekiel Emanuel: If You Want to Pay More for Your Doctor, You Can under Obamacare." The Washington Times. N.p., 8 Dec. 2013. Web. 30 Jan. 2015. <http://www.washingtontimes.com/news/2013/dec/8/dr-ezekiel-emanuel-if-you-want-pay-more-your-docto/>.

[12] "Obama: 'If You like Your Health Care Plan, You'll Be Able to Keep Your Health Care Plan'" Politifact. Tampa Bay Times, n.d.

Web. 30 Jan. 2015. <http://www.politifact.com/obama-like-health-care-keep/>.

[13] "Obama Statements on Single-payer Have Changed a Bit." Politifact. Tampa Bay Times, n.d. Web. 30 Jan. 2015. <http://www.politifact.com/truth-o-meter/statements/2009/jul/16/barack-obama/obama-statements-single-payer-have-changed-bit/>.

[14] United States Congress. House of Representatives. Transcript of Pelosi, House Democratic Leaders' Press Availability Today on Health Insurance Reform. Democratic Leader Nancy Pelosi. N.p., 5 Jan. 2010. Web. 30 Jan. 2015. <http://www.democraticleader.gov/newsroom/pelosi-house-democratic-leaders-press-availability-on-health-insurance-reform/>.

– CHAPTER EIGHT –

[1] "Meet the Founder." Turning Point USA. N.p., n.d. Web. 11 Feb. 2015. <http://www.turningpointusa.net/charliekirk/>.

[2] Baker, Peter, and David Herszenhorn. "Obama Signs Bill on Student Loans and Health Care." The New York Times. The New York Times Company, 30 Mar. 2010. Web. 11 Feb. 2015. <http://thecaucus.blogs.nytimes.com/2010/03/30/obama-signs-bill-on-student-loans-health-care/?_r=1>.

[3] "About Turning Point USA." Turning Point USA. N.p., n.d. Web. 11 Feb. 2015. <http://www.turningpointusa.net/aboutus/>.

[4] Jamrisko, Michelle, and Ilan Kolet. "College Tuition Costs Soar: Chart of the Day." Bloomberg Business. Bloomberg L.P., 18 Aug. 2014. Web. 11 Feb. 2015.

<http://www.bloomberg.com/news/articles/2014-08-18/college-tuition-costs-soar-chart-of-the-day>.

[5] Light, Joe. "First-Time Home Buyers Fade Further." The Wall Street Journal. Dow Jones & Company, 3 Nov. 2014. Web. 11 Feb. 2015. <http://www.wsj.com/articles/first-time-home-buyers-decline-in-u-s-1415036020>.

[6] Galston, William A. "Welcome to the Well-Educated-Barista Economy." The Wall Street Journal. Dow Jones & Company, 29 Apr. 2014. Web. 11 Feb. 2015. <http://www.wsj.com/articles/SB10001424052702303939404579530 230397152314>.

[7] "Student-loan Reform Slid into Health Law." The Washington Times. The Washington Times, LLC, 29 Mar. 2010. Web. 11 Feb. 2015. <http://www.washingtontimes.com/news/2010/mar/29/student-loan-takeover-slips-through-with-health-ca/?page=all.>.

[8] Lorin, Janet. "College Tuition in the U.S. Again Rises Faster Than Inflation." Bloomberg Business. Bloomberg L.P., 13 Nov. 2014. Web. 11 Feb. 2015. <http://www.bloomberg.com/news/articles/2014-11-13/college-tuition-in-the-u-s-again-rises-faster-than-inflation>.

[9] Rayfield, Nicholas. "National Student Loan Debt Reaches a Bonkers $1.2 Trillion." USA TODAY. Gannett Company, Inc., 08 Apr. 2015. Web. 11 Feb. 2015. <http://college.usatoday.com/2015/04/08/national-student-loan-debt-reaches-a-bonkers-1-2-trillion/>.

[10] Anderson, Nick. "Student Loan Default Rate Declines to 13.7 Percent; Federal Government Says the Figure 'is Still Too High'" The Washington Post. N.p., 24 Sept. 2014. Web. 11 Feb. 2015. <http://www.washingtonpost.com/local/education/national-student-

loan-default-rate-declines-to-137-percent/2014/09/24/d280c8bc-43ee-11e4-b437-1a7368204804_story.html>.

[11] Shin, Laura. "Average Student Loan Debt Rises, Tops $30,000 In 6 States." Forbes. N.p., 17 Nov. 2014. Web. 11 Feb. 2015. <http://www.forbes.com/sites/laurashin/2014/11/17/average-student-loan-debt-rises-tops-30000-in-6-states/>.

– CHAPTER NINE –

[1] Gilmore, Jim. "J. Kirk Wiebe." PBS. WGBH Educational Foundation, 13 Dec. 2013. Web. 14 Feb. 2015. <http://www.pbs.org/wgbh/pages/frontline/government-elections-politics/united-states-of-secrets/the-frontline-interview-j-kirk-wiebe/>.

[2] U.S. Code, § 5-3331. Print.

[3] Truman, Harry. "Communications Intelligence Activities." Presidential Memorandum. The White House. October 24, 1952. <https://www.nsa.gov/public_info/_files/truman/truman_memo.pdf>.

[4] "Bio: William Binney and J. Kirk Wiebe." Government Accountability Project. N.p., n.d. Web. 14 Feb. 2015. <http://whistleblower.org/bio-william-binney-and-j-kirk-wiebe>.

[5] Gilmore, Jim. "J. Kirk Wiebe." PBS. WGBH Educational Foundation, 13 Dec. 2013. Web. 14 Feb. 2015. <http://www.pbs.org/wgbh/pages/frontline/government-elections-politics/united-states-of-secrets/the-frontline-interview-j-kirk-wiebe/>.

[6] "Bio: William Binney and J. Kirk Wiebe." Government Accountability Project. N.p., n.d. Web. 14 Feb. 2015. <http://whistleblower.org/bio-william-binney-and-j-kirk-wiebe>.

[7] Martin, James. "Thomas Drake: The Dark Side of Data and the NSA." CBS News. CBS Interactive, 10 June 2013. Web. 14 Feb. 2015. <http://www.cbsnews.com/news/thomas-drake-the-dark-side-of-data-and-the-nsa/>.

[8] "Bio: William Binney and J. Kirk Wiebe." Government Accountability Project. N.p., n.d. Web. 14 Feb. 2015. <http://whistleblower.org/bio-william-binney-and-j-kirk-wiebe>.

[9] Risen, James, and Eric Lichtblau. "Bush Lets U.S. Spy on Callers Without Courts." The New York Times. N.p., 16 Dec. 2005. Web. 14 Feb. 2015. <http%3A%2F%2Fwww.nytimes.com%2F2005%2F12%2F16%2Fpolitics%2Fbush-lets-us-spy-on-callers-without-courts.html%3F_r%3D0>.

[10] Gilmore, Jim. "J. Kirk Wiebe." PBS. WGBH Educational Foundation, 13 Dec. 2013. Web. 14 Feb. 2015. <http://www.pbs.org/wgbh/pages/frontline/government-elections-politics/united-states-of-secrets/the-frontline-interview-j-kirk-wiebe/>.

[11] U.S. Constitution. Amend. IV.

[12] "Exceptions to the Warrant Requirement." Nolo. N.p., n.d. Web. 14 Feb. 2015. <http://www.nolo.com/legal-encyclopedia/exceptions-the-warrant-requirement>.

[13] Risen, James, and Eric Lichtblau. "Bush Lets U.S. Spy on Callers Without Courts." The New York Times. N.p., 16 Dec. 2005. Web. 14 Feb. 2015. <http%3A%2F%2Fwww.nytimes.com%2F2005%2F12%2F16%2Fpolitics%2Fbush-lets-us-spy-on-callers-without-courts.html%3F_r%3D0>.

[14] Greenwald, Glenn. "NSA Collecting Phone Records of Millions of Verizon Customers Daily." The Guardian. Guardian News and Media Limited, 6 June 2013. Web. 14 Feb. 2015. <http%3A%2F%2Fwww.theguardian.com%2Fworld%2F2013%2Fjun%2F06%2Fnsa-phone-records-verizon-court-order>.

[15] "Metadata." BusinessDictionary.com. WebFinance, Inc., n.d. Web. 14 Feb. 2015. <http://www.businessdictionary.com/definition/metadata.html>.

[16] The White House. Statement by the President. N.p., 7 June 2013. Web. 14 Feb. 2015. <https://www.whitehouse.gov/the-press-office/2013/06/07/statement-president>.

[17] Gilmore, Jim. "J. Kirk Wiebe." PBS. WGBH Educational Foundation, 13 Dec. 2013. Web. 14 Feb. 2015. <http://www.pbs.org/wgbh/pages/frontline/government-elections-politics/united-states-of-secrets/the-frontline-interview-j-kirk-wiebe/>.

[18] Bamford, James. "The NSA Is Building the Country's Biggest Spy Center (Watch What You Say)." Wired.com. Conde Nast Digital, 15 Mar. 2012. Web. Feb.-Mar. 2015. <http://www.wired.com/2012/03/ff_nsadatacenter/>.

- CHAPTER TEN -

[1] "Amanda Collins: A Survivor's Story." NRA Women. National Rifle Association, n.d. Web. 14 Feb. 2015. <http://www.nrawomen.tv/refuse-to-be-a-victim/video/amanda-collins-a-survivor-s-story/list/refuse-to-be-a-victim-feature>.

[2] Grinberg, Emanuella. "Nevada Man Convicted of Raping, Strangling College Student." CNN. Cable News Network, n.d. Web.

18 June 2015.

<http://www.cnn.com/2010/CRIME/05/27/brianna.denison.verdict/>.

[3] "Amanda Collins: A Survivor's Story." NRA Women. National Rifle Association, n.d. Web. 14 Feb. 2015.

<http://www.nrawomen.tv/refuse-to-be-a-victim/video/amanda-collins-a-survivor-s-story/list/refuse-to-be-a-victim-feature>.

[4] Castle Rock v. Gonzales. United States Supreme Court. 27 June 2005. Print.

[5] "Columbine High School Shootings Fast Facts." CNN. Cable News Network, 6 May 2015. Web. 31 May 2015.

<http://www.cnn.com/2013/09/18/us/columbine-high-school-shootings-fast-facts/>.

[6] "Virginia Tech Shootings Fast Facts." CNN. Cable News Network, 13 Apr. 2015. Web. 1 May 2015.

<http://www.cnn.com/2013/10/31/us/virginia-tech-shootings-fast-facts/>.

[7] "6 Shot Dead, including Gunman, at Northern Illinois University." CNN. Cable News Network, 14 Feb. 2008. Web. 21 Feb. 2015.

<http://www.cnn.com/2008/US/02/14/university.shooting/>.

[8] Barron, James. "Children Were All Shot Multiple Times With a Semiautomatic, Officials Say." The New York Times. N.p., 15 Dec. 2012. Web. 30 Feb. 2015.

<http://www.nytimes.com/2012/12/16/nyregion/gunman-kills-20-children-at-school-in-connecticut-28-dead-in-all.html>.

[9] "Colorado Theater Shooting Fast Facts." CNN. Cable News Network, 26 Apr. 2015. Web. 1 May 2015.

<http://www.cnn.com/2013/07/19/us/colorado-theater-shooting-fast-facts/>.

[10] Starr, Barbara, Catherine Shoichet, and Pamela Brown. "Navy Yard Shooting Rampage: 12 Killed, Dead Suspect Identified." CNN. Cable News Network, 16 Sept. 2013. Web. 21 Feb. 2015. <http://www.cnn.com/2013/09/16/us/dc-navy-yard-gunshots/>.

[11] "Workplace Violence." Environmental Health and Safety. Virginia Tech, n.d. Web. 24 Feb. 2015. <http://www.ehss.vt.edu/programs/EPP_workplace.php>.

[12] "Amanda's Story." One Million United. N.p., n.d. Web. 24 Feb. 2015. <http://www.onemillionunited.com/amandas-law/>.

[13] Garrett, Wilson. "Rape Survivor on Gun Control: How Does Rendering Me Defenseless Protect You against a Violent Crime?" Glenn Beck. Mercury Radio Arts, 26 Feb. 2013. Web. 24 Feb. 2015. <http://www.glennbeck.com/2013/02/26/rape-survivor-on-gun-control-how-does-rendering-me-defenseless-protect-you-against-a-violent-crime/>.

– CHAPTER ELEVEN –

[1] Lathrope, Daniel J. Selected Federal Taxation Statutes and Regulations 2015. St. Paul: West Academic, 2014. Print.

[2] "The Ratification of the 16th Amendment." History, Art & Archives. United States House of Representatives, n.d. Web. 18 Feb. 2015. <http://history.house.gov/Historical-Highlights/1901-1950/The-ratification-of-the-16th-Amendment/>.

[3] Russell, Jason. "Look at How Many Pages Are in the Federal Tax Code." Washington Examiner. N.p., 15 Apr. 2015. Web. 1 May 2015. <http://www.washingtonexaminer.com/look-at-how-many-pages-are-in-the-federal-tax-code/article/2563032>.

Notes

[4] "Brief History of IRS." IRS. Internal Revenue Service, n.d. Web. 28 Feb. 2015. <http://www.irs.gov/uac/Brief-History-of-IRS>.

[5] "Form 1040, U.S. Individual Income Tax Return." IRS. Internal Revenue Service, n.d. Web. 28 Feb. 2015. <http://www.irs.gov/uac/Form-1040,-U.S.-Individual-Income-Tax-Return>.

[6] O'Donnell, Carl. "The Rockefellers: The Legacy Of History's Richest Man." Forbes. N.p., 11 July 2014. Web. 28 Feb. 2015. <http://www.forbes.com/sites/carlodonnell/2014/07/11/the-rockefellers-the-legacy-of-historys-richest-man/>.

[7] "Estate History." Biltmore. N.p., n.d. Web. 28 Feb. 2015. <http://www.biltmore.com/visit/biltmore-house-gardens/estate-history>.

[8] Gwyn-Williams, Gregory, Jr. "Obama Proposes More Taxes - But, Tax Code Is Already 13 Miles Long!" CNS News. Media Research Center, 12 Apr. 2013. Web. 28 Feb. 2015. <http://www.cnsnews.com/blog/gregory-gwyn-williams-jr/obama-proposes-more-taxes-tax-code-already-13-miles-long>.

[9] Sahadi, Jeanne. "Married with Kids vs. Singles: Who Pays Higher Taxes?" CNN Money. Cable News Network, 25 Apr. 2014. Web. 28 Feb. 2015. <http://money.cnn.com/2014/04/25/pf/taxes/parents-singles-federal-taxes/>.

[10] "ObamaCare Employer Mandate." Obamacare Facts. N.p., n.d. Web. 30 Jan. 2015. <http://obamacarefacts.com/obamacare-employer-mandate/>.

[11] Pomerleau, Kyle. "Corporate Income Tax Rates around the World, 2014." Tax Foundation. N.p., 20 Aug. 2014. Web. 18 Feb. 2015. <http://taxfoundation.org/article/corporate-income-tax-rates-around-world-2014>.

12 "How FAIRtax Works." FAIRtax. Americans for Fair Taxation, n.d. Web. 25 Mar. 2015. <https://fairtax.org/about/how-fairtax-works>.

13 "Frequently Asked Questions." FAIRtax. Americans for Fair Taxation, n.d. Web. 25 Mar. 2015. <https://fairtax.org/faq>.

– CHAPTER TWELVE –

1 Lincoln, Abraham. "House Divided." Illinois State Capitol, Springfield, Illinois. 16 June 1858. Abraham Lincoln Online. Web. 20 Mar. 2015. <http://www.abrahamlincolnonline.org/lincoln/speeches/house.htm>.

2 Barrabi, Thomas. "Martin Luther King Quotes: 21 Memorable Sayings For MLK Day 2015." International Business Times. IBT Media Inc., 19 Jan. 2015. Web. 28 Feb. 2015. <http://www.ibtimes.com/martin-luther-king-quotes-21-memorable-sayings-mlk-day-2015-1783820>.

3 Badger, Emily. "Why Riots Erupted in One of the Most Segregated Metro Regions in the Country." The Washington Post. N.p., 11 Aug. 2014. Web. 20 Mar. 2015. <http://www.washingtonpost.com/blogs/wonkblog/wp/2014/08/11/why-riots-erupted-in-one-of-the-most-segregated-metro-regions-in-the-country/>.

4 Brown, Emily. "Timeline: Michael Brown Shooting in Ferguson, Mo." USA Today. Gannett, 02 Dec. 2014. Web. 1 June 2015. <http://www.usatoday.com/story/news/nation/2014/08/14/michael-brown-ferguson-missouri-timeline/14051827/>.

5 Frizell, Sam. "Http://time.com/3519407/ferguson-michael-brown-darrel-wilson/." Time Magazine. Time Inc., 18 Oct. 2014. Web. 18

Notes

June 2015. <http%3A%2F%2Ftime.com%2F3519407%2Fferguson-michael-brown-darrel-wilson%2F>.

[6] Reilly, Ryan J. "2 Police Officers Shot During Ferguson Protest." The Huffington Post. TheHuffingtonPost.com, 12 Mar. 2015. Web. 2 May 2015. <http://www.huffingtonpost.com/2015/03/12/ferguson-officers-shot-_n_6852700.html>.

[7] "Timeline: Freddie Gray's Arrest, Death and the Aftermath." The Baltimore Sun. N.p., n.d. Web. 10 May 2015. <http://data.baltimoresun.com/news/freddie-gray/>.

[8] "Freddie Gray's Spinal Injury Suggests 'forceful Trauma,' Doctors Say." The Baltimore Sun. N.p., 21 Apr. 2015. Web. 1 May 2015. <http://www.baltimoresun.com/health/bs-hs-gray-injuries-20150420-story.html>.

[9] Terkel, Amanda. "Mike Pence Signs Revised Indiana 'Religious Freedom' Law." The Huffington Post. TheHuffingtonPost.com, 2 Apr. 2015. Web. 1 June 2015. <http://www.huffingtonpost.com/2015/04/02/mike-pence-religious-freedom_n_6996144.html>.

[10] Barbaro, Michael, and Erik Eckholm. "Indiana Law Denounced as Invitation to Discriminate Against Gays." The New York Times. N.p., 27 Mar. 2015. Web. 5 May 2015. <http://www.nytimes.com/2015/03/28/us/politics/indiana-law-denounced-as-invitation-to-discriminate-against-gays.html>.

[11] "Indiana Pizza Place -- Forced to Close Doors After Refusing to Cater Gay Weddings." TMZ. EHM Productions, Inc., 1 Apr. 2015. Web. 1 June 2015. <http://www.tmz.com/2015/04/01/memories-pizza-closes-indiana-deny-service-gay-wedding/>.

[12] Malewitz, Becky. "Memories Pizza Fund Tops $842,000." South Bend Tribune. N.p., 4 Apr. 2015. Web. 1 June 2015.

<http://www.southbendtribune.com/news/local/memories-pizza-fund-tops/article_4aa6d171-1a4d-5739-9190-172cd145a392.html>.
[13] Howerton, Jason. "Gay Woman Who Donated $20 to Christian-Owned Indiana Pizzeria Reveals Why She Took Bold Stand." TheBlaze. N.p., 6 Apr. 2015. Web. 1 May 2015. <http://www.theblaze.com/stories/2015/04/06/gay-woman-who-donated-20-to-christian-owned-indiana-pizzeria-reveals-why-she-took-bold-stand/>.
[14] "Respect." Dictionary.com. Dictionary.com LLC, n.d. Web. 1 May 2015. <http://dictionary.reference.com/browse/respect>.
[15] "Civility." Dictionary.com. Dictionary.com LLC, n.d. Web. 1 May 2015. <http://dictionary.reference.com/browse/civility?s=t>.

- CHAPTER THIRTEEN -

[1] "Glenn Beck: How He Recovered His Life and His Free Will." TODAY.com. N.p., 19 Jan. 2011. Web. 1 May 2015. <http://www.today.com/id/41142549/ns/today-today_books/t/glenn-beck-how-he-recovered-his-life-his-free-will/>.
[2] Schnall, Marianne. "'Growing and Giving': An Interview With Tony Robbins." The Huffington Post. TheHuffingtonPost.com, 7 Nov. 2014. Web. 18 Apr. 2015. <http://www.huffingtonpost.com/marianne-schnall/growing-and-giving-an-int_b_4218532.html>.

www.ingramcontent.com/pod-product-compliance
Lightning Source LLC
Chambersburg PA
CBHW062007280526
45787CB00005B/2006